Books by Eudora Welty

Eudora Welty

Writers' Reflections upon First Reading Welty

Eudora WELTY

Writers' Reflections upon First Reading Welty

—⁓—

Edited by

Pearl Amelia McHaney

d

Hill Street Press   Athens, Georgia

A HILL STREET PRESS BOOK

First printing

2 4 6 8 10 9 7 5 3 1

ISBN # 1-892514-16-8 (trade edition)
ISBN # 1-892514-17-6 (limited edition of 200 numbered and 26 lettered copies)

LIBRARY OF CONGRESS CARD CATALOG NUMBER: 98-75334

for

Eudora Alice Welty

on the occasion of her birthday

April 13, 1999

———

Hill Street Press is grateful to Harcourt Brace & Company for granting permission to reprint selected passages from published works by Eudora Welty.

Excerpt from "The Wide Net" in *The Wide Net and Other Stories*, copyright ©1942 and renewed 1970 by Eudora Welty, reprinted by permission of Harcourt Brace & Company.

Excerpt from *The Robber Bridegroom*, copyright ©1942 and renewed 1970 by Eudora Welty, illustrations copyright 1978 by Pennroyal Press, Inc., reprinted by permission of Harcourt Brace & Company.

Excerpt from "Petrified Man" in *A Curtain of Green and Other Stories*, copyright ©1941 and renewed 1967 by Eudora Welty, reprinted by permission of Harcourt Brace & Company.

Excerpts from "Powerhouse," "Death of a Traveling Salesman," "Why I Live at the P.O." in *A Curtain of Green and Other Stories*, copyright ©1941 and renewed 1969 by Eudora Welty, reprinted by permission of Harcourt Brace & Company.

Excerpts from "A Curtain of Green" in *A Curtain of Green and Other Stories*, copyright ©1938 and renewed 1966 by Eudora Welty, reprinted by permission of Harcourt Brace & Company.

Excerpts from "The Whole World Knows" and "June Recital" in *The Golden Apples*, copyright ©1947 and renewed 1975 by Eudora Welty, reprinted by permission of Harcourt Brace & Company.

Excerpt from "Shower of Gold" in *The Golden Apples*, copyright ©1948 and renewed 1976 by Eudora Welty, reprinted by permission of Harcourt Brace & Company.

Excerpt from "The Wanderers" in *The Golden Apples*, copyright ©1949 and renewed 1977 by Eudora Welty, reprinted by permission of Harcourt Brace & Company.

Thanks also to Harvard University Press for permission to use the quotation by Eudora Welty appearing on the back cover of this book from *One Writer's Beginnings*, copyright 1983 and renewed 1984 by Eudora Welty.

Contents

Preface

Why These Invitations?

*M*y first encounter with Eudora Welty came, as it did for many in this volume, when I was a college student, but I met her firsthand many years later in a brief shy encounter at her seventy-fifth birthday party, the April 1984 Southern Literary Festival at Millsaps College in Jackson. I have celebrated her birthday ever since, with friends, students, teachers, and visitors from abroad — dedicating cakes that set off the family smoke detector, hearing high school juniors declare with delight that they finally understood "A Worn Path," feeding Weltyan meals to college students equally hungry for the words she used to describe such feasts, helping a Japanese translator through some of the mysteries of Southern speech, or watching a usually quiet girl play her violin passionately in Eudora Welty's honor. Ten years after that first handshake, I helped the city of

Jackson, the University Press of Mississippi, Lemuria Books, and many friends celebrate Welty's eighty-fifth birthday with the publication of *A Writer's Eye: Collected Books Reviews*. I was the proud mid-wife and the work afforded me several dream-fulfilling afternoons of conversation with Miss Welty. More recently I have traveled again to Jackson to slip in Welty's door with greetings from many of those to whom her work means so much.

To begin this project as a celebration and tribute for her ninetieth birthday was, then, no unusual step, though it has been a remarkable one, thanks to the gifts of nearly two dozen writers who have come along to the party. I began by inviting several of Eudora's oldest friends, those with whom she often shares such milestones, and then her friends who have spoken so perceptively in homage to her life's work. I hoped for a modest party of nine, one for each decade, thinking to assemble them in the pages of the *Eudora Welty Newsletter*, which I began to edit at the beginning of its twenty-first year of publication. But as word of the celebration spread, Elizabeth Spencer suggested Alice Munro, and Lee Smith made me bold enough to invite Louis Rubin, and so it went. Soon I had twenty-two women and men eager to remind Eudora Welty—and all good readers—what the impact of a great writer can do to and for the mind of another writer, whether that other writer is already accomplished or just starting out.

So they gave into my keeping a volume of discerning reports of first encounters with and recollections of Eudora, a grand gathering for Eudora Welty's ninetieth birthday. The Welty stories and novels remembered and brought along by these writers add more company to the celebration: Phoenix Jackson, Edna Earle Ponder, Virgie and Katie Rainey, Cassie Morrison, Powerhouse, Sister, Mr. Bowman, Lily Daw and her three ladies, the Spanish guitarist. Distant guests are hailed: Thomas Mann, Elizabeth Bowen, Virginia Woolf. By way of demonstrating Welty's impact on readers who are not writers, Greg Johnson and Mary Hood bring their mothers to the party, as Reynolds Price, Lee Smith, and Fred Chappell bring their teachers. Eudora herself was the teacher for Ellen Gilchrist and Elizabeth Spencer, but then one realizes that, figuratively, she was the teacher for all who write here. We like to think that the author who has written so tellingly and perceptively about teachers will feel pleasure that this tribute says, among many ways of expressing love and gratitude, "Happy Birthday, Teacher."

All those invited here are writers, mostly of fiction, though to invite all of Welty's admirers in the writing trade alone was not possible. What these writers remind us, however, is that serious members of this rare guild, better than any others, have the greatest potential to understand and identify the achievement of a modest genius like Eudora Welty. The quality of mind, the power of imagination, the dedication to the inner life impart to them the nature of their craft, the philosophical import behind the reality that the common reader rarely perceives. As we know, when asked what it takes to become a great writer, great writers usually recommend the reading of other great writers. And even when great writers write with appreciation essays about the works they admire, rarely do they tell us everything they know or directly see. Rather, they speak of mystery, of surprise, of emotional import, of inspiration and kinship, or even of conversion. Gifts, such as those Eudora Welty received and has given to so many, come to those who will appreciate them, will understand how to use them—when they are ready.

For all the gifts Eudora Welty has let come our way, we thank her. Looked at from afar or from near at hand, Eudora's fiction and Eudora herself are young at ninety!

PEARL AMELIA MCHANEY

—៳៳—

I

Charm

We were in Chattanooga, at the
Conference on Southern Literature, and we were on an elevator going down. This was at the wonderful old Reed House
Hotel. There was a big reception down in the lobby of that
hotel. On the elevator it was Ms. Eudora, Ellen Douglas, and
myself, as I recall. Suddenly Eudora put her hand to her chest,
with a look of alarm on her face. I said, "What is it?" She said
"I forgot my name tag." Ellen Douglas and I exchanged an
amused look, and I said something like, "Ms. Eudora, there's
NOBODY at this thing that doesn't know exactly who you
are." And she said, very softly and sweetly, "Well, I still must
go back and get it." So we did.

I first read this wonderful writer when I was in my late twen-
ties—I admired the stories very much, as everyone does, of

course; but it wasn't until I read *The Ponder Heart*, in 1975, that I realized the redemptive quality of her writing. That book, with its marvelously tolerant and forbearing voice, literally called me back from the abyss. What I remember is that I had had a crisis where I began to fear for my sanity; in my then very confused and anxiety-laden head, there convened a judge and jury, which accused me at every turn my mind took. I could not convince myself that my own thoughts, unruly as they were, and often purely crazy, were not evidence of what I feared, that I was losing my mind. Something in that wonderful novel, Edna Earle's attitude about all that, her tolerance of the confusion of mind, the fact that it contains ridiculous and dreadful contradictions—that is how I remember it anyway—something in it caused the judge and jury to be disbanded, and I could feel it dispersing, adjourning, as I read on. I remember more the feeling of having been healed, reading that book, than very many of the details of the book itself.

It's been more than twenty years. But the feeling remains, and the sense of gratitude to Eudora remains, too. I had the pleasure of telling her this at a party one afternoon, when she and I were the only people there drinking bourbon. Eudora and I had a delightful hour, in which we also agreed that her line "If you're so smart, why ain't you rich?" from "Petrified Man" absolutely ALSO belongs at the end of Flannery O'Connor's great story "Good Country People." We had a good laugh about that.

And I guess the one most important element of this great person's whole being is CHARM. It is in everything she has ever written or done.

RICHARD BAUSCH

—∿—

II

Tough as Fire

*I*f you enter our house by the
front door, you will immediately see the photographs of two
women: Flannery O'Connor and Eudora Welty. They were
framed by and presented as a gift from Elizabeth Evans, retired
head of the Georgia Tech English Department, whose book on
Eudora Welty appeared in 1981. In the top photo, Miss Welty
is seated, chin on hand, the back of her head reflected in a mir-
ror; she strikes a similar pose in a much younger snapshot on the
book cover of her collected correspondence with her agent (and
mine) Diarmuid Russell. In both photos she avoids the lens,
gazing down and off to her right, pensive. But my framed one
shows her in her own home at age seventy-five, looking so self-
contained and serene that photographer Mark Morrow might
well be absent.

Each time I climb the stairs to the computer to write, it is a salutary—even daunting—experience to pass the sidelong gazes of these two writers.

Miss Welty's likeness is located on top by seniority, born sixteen years earlier, but also because her fiction is kinder. O'Connor sounded defensive in an early letter denying she was "one of the subtle, sensitive writers like Eudora Welty." Despite the age difference, when O'Connor died in 1964, much of Welty's best known and steadily ripening work lay still ahead.

From Welty's mature face may be inferred the very synthesis she once ascribed to Henry Green: "A life's confidence is what you feel you have been given."

O'Connor did not discover Welty's stories until she attended graduate school. My admiration was delayed until college, too, since most high school texts preferred O. Henry's surprise endings, so *The Golden Apples* was a revelation—not so much because Morgana, Mississippi, seemed a real Delta town but because its inhabitants exceeded reality. If O'Connor believed Georgia, like Israel, was a wide enough stage for acting out great religious drama, Miss Welty made those early extended family stories expand into the mythological. The two women writers were very different in content, though alike in their reach, their sense of huge scale. Anne Tyler has emphasized the strength of Welty's method by noting that her stories are concerned "less with what happens than with whom it happens *to*."

Now it is sixty-three years since her first story was published, and ninety years since Eudora Welty was born in Jackson, Mississippi, to a schoolteacher and an insurance salesman—parents she has consistently honored and thanked. By example, she is living *dis*proof of the neurotic artist, maintaining a quiet and productive life while fulfilling domestic and family duties, accepting honors modestly, reading and commenting on her contemporaries, and at last distilling the rich essence of that admirable interior life in *One Writer's Beginnings.* When one interviewer wondered if she might have preferred marriage instead of adventure, she responded that "all experience is an enrichment instead of an impoverishment." She has influenced generations of writers while her lucid and luminous prose defies imitation. An e-mail computer program bears her name. Her photographs constitute a metaphor for her story-method, since it was at the camera she first learned "to wait" for "the moment in which people reveal themselves."

Though I never met O'Connor, Miss Welty did come to the University of North Carolina-Chapel Hill to honor Louis Rubin—and here she revealed herself.

I was assigned to chauffeur her from the Carolina Inn to Memorial Hall where she would deliver her address. All day it rained heavily. I thought nervously of the risk of skids, hydroplaning, drunk drivers. I acquired umbrellas, plastic hats, tarpaulins. To each of my phone calls to set a pickup time, Miss

Welty said she was still revising her speech. I knew she was said to lay out pieces of a story on her dining room table and pin and re-pin as with a dress pattern. The rains intensified; time passed. I could visualize headlines: LOCAL SCRIBBLER KILLS FIRST LADY OF LETTERS IN STUPID WRECK.

At last I went to wait and pace in the Inn lobby. Suddenly, a fire alarm sounded. I rushed to the desk—Miss Welty's room? Quick, quickly!

The clerk said the alarm had doubtless been set off by a mere cigarette smoker. He did not give out room numbers. The alarm and downpour kept on.

Then a siren sounded; a fire truck braked at the main entrance, and firemen in yellow suits dashed in, carrying tanks. This time I grabbed hold of the desk clerk. (New headline: FIRE KILLS FIRST LADY OF LETTERS WHILE FOOLS DO NOTHING.) I told him Miss Welty was no spring chicken; she was probably frail; we needed to—

And then Eudora Welty appeared. Not even winded. She had, of course, remembered not to use an elevator in the event of fire, but to get herself (and her speech) down the regular stairs.

Frail? After delivering an excellent speech to a crowded auditorium, she was willing to remain onstage signing books (unlike many younger, self-important writers we've entertained). The lines were long; her awed readers and fans verbose. I waited to one side with my unused umbrellas, plastic hats, and tarpaulins. I was tired. She did not seem to be.

After a very long time, one of Welty's last admirers stepped forward and held out a handful of limp vegetation. I saw that the offering was largely wilted Queen Anne's lace from a roadside. The woman blew out on one breath: "I've come all the way from Asheville to say how much you mean . . . "

And as quickly and smoothly as reflex, Miss Welty said, "Oh my dear!" and gave the young woman a series of pats on the arm. As if taking orchids, she then accepted the scraggly bouquet in her left hand, admired it, and, with her right, wrote a personal message above her signature.

Happy Birthday, Miss Eudora Welty—tough under fire, tender enough to turn weeds into orchids.

And every time I pass your photograph I'll remember what Alice Walker wrote after she visited you in Jackson: "Life has made a face for her that concentrates a beauty in her eyes."

DORIS BETTS

III

First Encounters

The first encounter with Eudora Welty's work came while I was lying in Mission Hospital in Asheville, North Carolina, recovering from an automobile accident that crushed my right hip. It was a lengthy convalescence and I received numerous books as gifts. One was a trade paperback edition of *The Golden Apples*, given me by one of my mother's friends. She had not read the volume herself but had heard that it was "genuinely literary." Why she suspected that the genuinely literary would hold any interest for me I cannot say. I was fifteen years old: Shakespeare was literary, but Ray Bradbury was a *great author*.

The first story I read was "Music from Spain" and I read it without any knowledge of who Andrés Segovia was. Nevertheless, I knew for a certainty that the grand, bumbling guitarist in the story was drawn after a real figure; a completely fictional character would not retain such mystery. I found "Music" mesmerizing. I didn't know what it meant—I still don't. If I were forced to describe its subject matter, I might say it is a portrait of the artist as being a part of the world and yet at the same time outside it, a somnambulist, if you will, and I would define that word as a "dream-walker." The theme of the story I might identify as the transfiguration of ordinary life by the power of art.

But I wouldn't seriously defend these speculations, for in truth, this story remains for me—like "Powerhouse," that other magnificent story of a musician—ineffable, as ineffable as the music it celebrates. I think ineffability was a large part of Eudora's intention in writing it; she wanted to produce that peculiar effect that music engenders on the spirit, of having an undeniable experience, a profound experience, that truly cannot be meaningfully described in any terms other than itself. A number of poems achieve this effect—most notably perhaps, Coleridge's "Kubla Khan"—but precious few pieces of fiction do, and the fact that Eudora has written a half dozen of them is one of the reasons she is so admired by other writers.

She always has been admired by writers, long before she gained her present dreadnought fame. In the spring of 1962, she visited Duke University where I was lodged as a graduate student. My anxious friend, Dr. William Blackburn, most heartily desired for me to make a close acquaintance with Eudora; it was one of his many elaborate designs to further my literary career. He had engineered it so that I would walk with our esteemed author from her rooms to the dining hall where a luncheon was to be held. This was a distance of about half a mile and when the late May day dawned hot and humid, I realized that such a trek would not be pleasant for Eudora in her high heels. Having no car at that time, I telephoned another literary guest, the poet X. J. Kennedy. "Joe," I said, "I've got a little problem. Would you mind giving Eudora Welty and me a ride to lunch today?"

"Not at all," he said. "Should I also make room for Thomas Mann?"

FRED CHAPPELL

—ᴍ—

IV

On the Occasion of Eudora Welty's

Ninetieth Birthday

*I*f I were to write an account of my very first reading of Eudora Welty, I would be lying: I don't recall which of her stories I first read, only the delight of discovery. My thoughts about her work and her life have a focus different from introduction, I recall, rather, *connections*.

I recall reading *The Robber Bridegroom*—it must have been when I was in my late teens—and being blown away by the extraordinary discovery that a fairy tale could be acted out in the very forest and along the very river where I'd spent my most vividly remembered childhood days. And the Trace—the Natchez Trace—whose history I had picked up in dabs and snatches from grandparents and parents talking of treks overland from

Nashville, of vanished great-great uncles, of barges and bandits and gypsies and Indians and beleaguered settlers.

I read: "Away out in the woods from Rodney's Landing, in a clearing in the live-oaks and the cedars and the magnolia trees, with the Mississippi River a mile to the back and the Old Natchez Trace a mile to the front, was the house Clement Musgrove had built. . . ." Surely, I thought, Miss Welty must have read the tales my grandmother wrote and read aloud to us as children—fairy tales set in the recognizable woods around her home, in which ranzeboos (mysterious, clever, tree-dwelling creatures) swung down from the live-oak trees and rescued Niparette (a much put-upon heroine) from galloping cotton backs and wicked, near-sighted aunts for whom she was forced to thread thousands of needles.

The deeper connection, constant throughout the book, reaches its most passionate statement in Clement's wonderful elegy beginning, "But the time of cunning has come . . . and my time is over, for cunning is of a world I will have no part in. Two long ripples are following down the Mississippi behind the approaching somnolent eyes of the alligator. . . . Men are following men down the Mississippi, hoarse and arrogant by day, wakeful and dreamless by night. . . ."

I saw that Miss Welty had found a way to use myth and fairy tale to engage us with our beautiful, guilt-ridden, tragic home. All Southern writers have had to deal with history, with race—white writers with guilt, black writers with rage. And we must deal, too, like writers from other parts of the country, with the rape of our land, the brutality of frontier life, the destruction of Native American culture, and the greed for gold of our money-driven world. Through playfulness, through mythologizing, through a kind of bloody and ruthless comedy, Welty had made a profound statement about the fate of our country, a statement with which I could not but connect.

"In the sky is the perpetual wheel of buzzards. A circle of bandits counts out the gold, with bending shoulders more slaves mount the block and go down, a planter makes a gesture of abundance with his riding whip, a flatboatman falls back from the tavern door to the river below with scarcely time for a splash, a rope descends from a tree and curls into a noose. . . ."

I can scarcely resist continuing to quote: " 'All I must do is cut off his head,' said the Little Harp. 'Then I can take his place. Advancement is only a matter of swapping heads about.'"

Perhaps it was *The Robber Bridegroom* with which I made the first connection, but perhaps not. It may have been "A Worn Path." I recall reading and rereading the stories in *A Curtain of Green*, particularly "A Worn Path" and "Powerhouse," and of connecting with, learning from the language. Or perhaps I should say marveling at rather than learning from. Again, it seemed to me, the language transformed, raised to a new intensity, the land I lived in, the people I had heard speak.

"Lying on my back like a June-bug waiting to be turned over" old Phoenix says, and "I don't see no two-headed snake coming around that tree," and ". . . who be you the ghost of? For I have heard of nary death close by." It's a voice I seem always to have known.

And "Powerhouse," the very personification of the nature of art:

> "[H]e took hold of the piano, as if he saw it for the first time in his life, and tested it for strength, hit it down in the bass, played an octave with his elbow, lifted the top, looked inside, and leaned against it with all his might. He sat down and played it for a few minutes with outrageous force and got it under his power—a bass deep and coarse as a sea net— then produced something glimmering and fragile, and smiled."

This is Powerhouse. It's also Eudora Welty, who produced a body of work as deep and coarse as a sea net—and then produced something glimmering and fragile. Whose piano is our language and our lives. Who hands us the gift of her work and smiles.

ELLEN DOUGLAS

—⁓—

V

Out of the Wilderness

I grew up in western North Carolina in a town of three thousand people. For over half of my life I thought a bagel was a small dog. I wanted to be a writer, but believed that writers were creatures only slightly less divine than angels—except that, instead of heaven, writers lived in New York City or England. And because I was a good Baptist boy, fatalistic the way good Baptist boys are raised to be, I figured I had a better shot at becoming an angel than I did of becoming a writer, which is to say: not much. I was as sure that I had nothing to write about, that I didn't know a story worth telling, as I was sure my heart was black with sin.

And then, in the fall of 1979, I was led out of the wilderness by a voice. I was a freshman in college, reading at my desk. The voice said: "Papa-Daddy! Sister says she fails to understand why you don't cut off your beard." The voice, of course, belonged to Eudora Welty, channeled through the character of Sister in the story "Why I Live at the P.O." and as is often the case with voices that lead people out of the wilderness, I didn't believe at first what I had heard: incredibly, the voice had the same accent I did. It was the first time I had realized that literature could speak in the language I recognized as my own. When, just to make sure, I said, "Excuse me?" the voice said: "You ought to see Mama, she weighs two hundred pounds and has real tiny feet."

Sister's/Welty's voice is one of the most imitated in all of American literature. It is most often poorly imitated because on the surface it appears to be a thing more placid and simple than it turns out to be—like a pond that conceals an alligator. I am only now beginning to understand its great subtlety and depth of characterization. At first I responded to the story selfishly, on a decidedly primitive level, the way a chimp, in order to receive a reward, might match a picture of a food it likes with the food itself. Sister's family reminded me of people I had known forever; Sister and Mama and Stella-Rondo and Uncle Rondo and Papa-Daddy could have been members of my church. This simple matching of the world pointed me toward what seems to me now an obvious thought: if characters who resembled the people I knew could inhabit a story, then why not those people themselves? That short leap of logic, unimpressive though it may be, gave me the secret courage to consider the previously blasphemous thought that my small world might turn out to be a writer's world after all. And it was like waking up.

"Why I Live at the P.O." eventually led me not only to Welty's other stories, but to the work of William Faulkner and Lee Smith and Fred Chappell and Kaye Gibbons, all Southerners whose backgrounds were no more remarkable than—or as remarkable as—my own. That I've been able to write stories into which strangers can look and perhaps see their own reflections still seems to me a miracle—a miracle that began twenty years ago when I looked into the second smallest post office in the state of Mississippi and saw myself. In all that time, "Why I Live at the P.O." has never lost its miraculous sheen; it has remained for me a type of sacred text, its author a kind of human angel.

As a former Baptist, I understand that a personal testimony is relevant and appropriate only if—by documenting a representative experience—it glorifies a greater power. The greater power here is Eudora Welty's. In "Why I Live at the P.O." I found a small salvation and a personal promised land, but that is less than incidental to the story's main message: the human voice crying out, no matter how small or far away, is always worthy of attention.

TONY EARLEY

—✺—

—✺—

VI

Head Stung, Heart Stung

*L*ast Sunday, September 20, 1998, while I was outside, clearing brush, a yellow jacket stung me between the eyes. Jolted, I came inside, took two Advil. Next morning I was pretty much over it.

About twenty years ago, on the night of May 14, 1978, I saw and heard Eudora Welty read "Why I Live at the P.O." on public television. Jolted, shaken, taken—stung, but without pain—I went straight to my journal and wrote, "Tomorrow, May 15, 1978, I will get up and start writing fiction seriously." I got up next morning and started writing fiction seriously. I'm still not over it.

—⁓—

In 1973, just after we met, Susan Ketchin and I talked for hours about music, family, flying, education (we were graduate students in English Education) and literature. I was a fan of Hemingway, Twain, Crane, Thoreau, and New Journalism. She was passionate about Faulkner, O'Connor, and Welty.

"You haven't read those people?" Susan asked.

I hadn't. And I didn't see any rush. I was on the way to being a professor of education. I had Dewey, Kozol, Mills, Schlechty, Sol Worth. I was going to write about English teaching methods, about using film in the classroom, about organizational norms in schools, about learning theory.

"You haven't read those people?" Susan asked again.

"No."

"You should."

—⁂—

My advisor and main professor, Sterling Hennis—for whom I was a graduate assistant—taught future English teachers to use reader's theater in the classroom. A short story would be turned into a script and students would rehearse from the script, and then, still using the script, perform the story before a live audience or perhaps record it on audio tape. His student teachers practiced what he preached. One asked me to read the Misfit's part for an audio production of the short story, "A Good Man Is Hard to Find." "Who wrote that?" I asked Susan.

"Flannery O'Connor."

"Oh."

Then I was asked to play the part of Papa Daddy in a reader's theater adaptation of the short story, "Why I Live at the P.O." The script was funny. Each time we rehearsed it, it got funnier. It got to be so funny, so good, and so exactly human, I asked, "Who wrote that?"

"Eudora Welty."

"Oh."

Susan and I were married in 1975. She was teaching high school English—and guitar on the side. I was writing a dissertation about "visual dialects" in film, supervising student teachers, taking graduate education courses. I graduated in 1977, got a college teaching job, and had my first research paper rejected.

Susan and I and several friends formed a reader's theater group. Our first production was "Why I Live at the P. O." This time, I played Uncle Rondo, Susan played Stella-Rondo. Then I played Papa-Daddy again. Then I played Mama. I could not get enough of the story—written by this Eudora Welty.

Susan and I started quoting lines from "the P.O." (We still do.) I'd suddenly say "Burdyburdyburdyburdy." She would be watching TV and say, "Not even the grace to get up off the bed."

"Why I Live at the P.O." was still getting funnier, even more cherished. The characters were visible, alive, audible. I was there in it all. It was becoming more than a story. It was becoming a presence in my life. It was almost a child, a human being, a friend. Even so, I hadn't really given the author, Eudora Welty, much thought.

I began playing around writing fiction. I started a war story, something with a hero. It fizzled. I started a story about a summer camp for retarded children. Fizzled. It dawned on me that "Why I Live at the P.O." was about my people. It was like a relative. Could my life—my life growing up—be worthy of fiction? I wasn't sure. The fiction I'd read and loved was about big game hunting, war, and the nonfiction tended toward philosophy.

During Christmas vacation of that first semester as a college professor, 1977, I started writing a story about a boy falling through his kitchen floor into an open well in the crawl space. I used my own life in it, my memories, family memories—my people. I read "Petrified Man." I read "Keela, the Outcast Indian Maiden." I saw every scene, heard every word. These stories were working on me, changing me—I didn't exactly know how or why. But I had given little thought to their author. I had no idea of her voice, her presence, her beauty.

And then on the night of May 14, 1978, I turned on the television. There she was. The author. She was beautiful, composed. She started reading in a voice strung with gold and blackberries: "I was getting along fine with Mama, Papa-Daddy and Uncle Rondo until my sister Stella-Rondo just separated from her husband and came back home again." That author's presence was magic, her voice—music. I was stung through the heart. It didn't hurt a bit. It felt good. The experience stays bigger in my life than much else:

That one story read aloud by that one writer.

CLYDE EDGERTON

—ɯ—

VII

Miss Eudora When Last Seen

*I*t would have been in late 1947 or early 1948, most likely the latter because there is a blizzard in the story and I remember the blizzard as being early in the new year (1948).

Anyway, the War was over and I had gone north to go to college (Princeton) and, except for football season during which I was trying and pretending to be a player, I spent as much time as I could in New York City, an hour away from Princeton. I had friends there, grown-ups who were fun to be with and one of them was a beautiful painter from my hometown who was kind and hospitable. I went to see her as often as I could in those days.

At Princeton I had just discovered Southern literature. I had my brand new, neat, fat little Viking *Portable Faulkner* which was my prize possession. I also had a paperback copy of Carson McCullers's *The Heart Is a Lonely Hunter*, given to me by the painter.

I had not yet heard of Eudora Welty, but on a weekend in the City I found and bought two of her books—*A Curtain of Green* (1941) and *The Wide Net* (1943). I missed *The Robber Bridegroom* (1942) which would later (soon enough) become my absolute special favorite, and I missed *Delta Wedding* (1946), too, at that time.

I bought the two story collections on the weekend of the big blizzard just as the first few harmless flakes were falling. It would have to be late Friday afternoon, then. I did not buy the books at the Gotham Book Mart as you might expect. I can't give you the name of the store. It was new and fancy and Swedish (I think), somewhere among the other bright and new and fancy facades of Fifth Avenue or maybe Madison. They had mostly art books for sale. Only a few, a very few, literary items in stock. I browsed, picked up a Welty, opened at random, read a couple or three sentences and knew at once and for sure that I wanted everything they had, up to the limits of the cash I was carrying, by this Welty person.

Bought those books and read and re-read them, with enormous pleasure and excitement, that very weekend when I was, finally, snowbound in a walk-up apartment, albeit with good company, in Greenwich Village. At some point a small group of us, painters and musicians and the college kid, walked in fresh knee-deep snow up the middle of Fifth Avenue. Except for us it was almost empty, only a few people darkly wrapped against the cold and no vehicles, nary a one, of any kind, not even a snow plough. Back inside, the little apartment warmed in places by the burners of a gas cooking stove, I curled up with Eudora Welty. Changed my life and changed my luck (as they say). As a reader—I knew then and there that I would be reading and re-reading her work the rest of my life with joy and undiminishing excitement. And as a writer—because that is what I had always wanted to be if I couldn't be a fireman, a steeplejack or a loco-motive engineer—she opened doors and windows for me, set an impeccable example, not to be *copied* (which I couldn't even if I wanted and tried to), but to admire and strive to be worthy of. Which did not mean, then or now, that I sought her approval for my work, which (as you'll see a little later) I could not have earned in any case if that had been my wish. Instead, and much more important to a learning writer, she challenged me, and any other new writer, young or old, challenged us all to do nothing less than our best.

What about technique? you might well ask. You know, tricks of the trade.

Well now, that's another story. Of course, there are good things of the kind that any writer can learn from close study of Welty's work. No doubt. But the truth is, the truly amazing thing, that again and again in her stories (novels too) there is a totally inexplicable moment of pure unadulterated and inimitable magic. I mean real magic, because there is no technical or mechanical explanation for it. Take a good look sometime at that great story, "Powerhouse," I dare you, and see if you can really figure out how she did it, how she got from here to there and back.

If it is magic, then what can the writer learn? Answer: to work without ceasing and to be ready, always, for the arrival of angels and magic when and if they elect to come. You can learn technique from lesser beings. You learn craft from honest and honorable craftsmen. From a few, the very few, including Eudora Welty, you learn to recognize and rejoice in art when you see it. From Eudora Welty, you learn to believe in magic.

I knew all that and more after my snowbound weekend with two books by Eudora Welty.

—m—

I have been with Eudora Welty in person on a number of occasions, at a number of conferences, celebrations, panels, and so forth, mostly down South, though once in far-off North Dakota. (What we were all doing *there*, I can't imagine.) And it has always been a great pleasure, thanks to her generous and gracious manner, her wit and good humor, her integrity and her sharp tongue. For this latter she has not been sufficiently credited. Call it part of a tough-minded vision. She is not in the least sentimental, in life or art. She is unfailing in her compassion for others.

I was not, have never been one of her good and close friends, in a social sense. It seemed from day one until now that she was spoken for (as they say). There were many other writers—William Jay Smith, Walker Percy, Reynolds Price, Peter Taylor, Richard Ford, Barry Hannah—who were around and about her in a social sense as good friends. She didn't need another writer in her train. If she ever did, of course, I would have swallowed shyness and abjured my clumsiness and done my dead-level best to serve.

Way back when, when my first collection of stories, *King of the Mountain*, was published, somebody, a mutual friend, sent her a copy. Shortly thereafter she sent him a postcard thanking him, saying she had much enjoyed the first story in the book, "The Rivals," and was looking forward to the others. I didn't hear from him again for a good while, years in fact. When I did run into him somewhere, I asked if he had ever heard any more from Miss Welty about the rest of the book. "Too much ugly talk," he said. "She said there was too much ugly talk in some of the others." Were my feelings hurt? Not a bit. I was charmed and enchanted. I knew well enough the stories she referred to; they were my Army stories and in some of them people did indeed indulge in "ugly talk." My mother, a few years older than Eudora Welty, agreed with Welty about that, though being a Southern mother, she defended me without stint or hesitation in her book club and her bridge club.

Truth is, I wouldn't have sent the book to Miss Welty myself. It seemed an imposition and I saw and still see no good reason why she should have to read stories (be they good or bad or indifferent) about tacky people in the U.S. Army. You could look at it this way: One of the reasons we were in the U.S. Army was to spare people like Miss Welty and my mother from the ugly talk of an ugly world.

With a little age and experience, I probably wouldn't have wanted to shock folks with my Army stories. With some wisdom, I might have realized that I couldn't shock them anyway. They (and she) knew the world as well or better than I.

Many years later, with panels and conferences and such in between, I enjoyed a most pleasant time in her company when she came to Charlottesville to visit old friends and, while she was here, to give a reading to raise some money for a literacy program. It was arranged for four of us to read on the program—myself, Rita Mae Brown, Ann Beattie and, the featured star, Miss Welty. I read first and as briefly as possible, something from one of the Elizabethan novels with not a smidgin of ugly talk. Read and sat down next to Miss Welty, noticing that she had a copy of the Modern Library edition of *Selected Stories of Eudora Welty* in hand. It was somewhat battered and certainly well-thumbed. From time to time, she stole a glance at it, checking the text. She was, I was pleased to notice, as nervous as the rest of us, really, maybe more so. After all this time. After years of reading to audiences. I took it as an act of duty, assumed that she didn't really enjoy standing up and showing off her art and craft—but there was nothing but to do it.

The story she was glancing at, from time to time, was "A Worn Path." The margins were marked with little notes to herself. I'm pretty sure that one read: "Slow Down!"

Rita Mae Brown rose and read something that was supposed to be funny and did, indeed, arouse some laughter in the audience. Miss Welty, next to me, sighed a deep sigh. Then Ann Beattie rose and read a very funny piece evoking much laughter. In the midst of this, Miss Welty sighed a deeper sigh and then began riffling pages, looking for something. Just as Ann Beattie finished, Miss Welty found "Why I Live at the P.O.," rose and moved to the lectern to read it. Over her head, like a balloon in a comic strip, I saw clearly the entirely imaginary words—"You girls want to be funny. I'll give you funny." And it was wonderfully funny, the best I've ever heard her read it. The audience was, as they say, in stitches.

Later that weekend, the president of the University of Virginia gave a luncheon for Miss Welty at the French House where they practice the French language and lifestyle. Various students and faculty (including lucky me) were invited. It was a really good meal with great wines and conversation and went on into the middle of the afternoon. It was there that I learned Miss Welty was blessed with a hearty appetite, worthy of one of our football players if truth has to be known. She was about to eat a second dessert when her host and friend spoke up. "Eudora," he said. "It's after three already and we are due for dinner at Monticello at five or five-thirty. . . ."

"Five-thirty!" she said. "By five-thirty I'll be hungry as a bear."

—∞—

I am happy to join in this tribute and celebration for the ninetieth birthday of Eudora Welty. She and her work have been part of my life for half a century. Which, while it can't compete with ninety, is still a big chunk of time. Consider: How many writers have kept your attention and given you nothing but joy for fifty years?

The last time I saw Miss Welty was at a meeting of the Fellowship of Southern Writers (of which she is a charter member) in Chattanooga where she was to receive an award. More or less by accident it fell my duty and pleasure to escort her onto the stage, from backstage, at the theater where the ceremony took place. With Miss Welty holding my arm, we stepped out of shadowy darkness into a sudden blinding blaze of light and an animal roar of applause. The crowd, a couple of thousand or more, was on its feet cheering and clapping.

"How do you like this, Miss Welty?" I asked

She gave me a brief and lovely smile.

"If they keep it up," she said, "I just might have to cry."

We are going to keep it up, Miss Welty.

GEORGE GARRETT

—∞—

—∞—

VIII

A Piece of News

When I was twenty-seven years old I read in the Jackson newspaper that Eudora Welty was going to teach at Millsaps College and that selected *writers* were going to be allowed to study with her. I didn't know who Eudora Welty was. I had been gone from Mississippi for many years and had only come back now and then to visit. I had only been living in Jackson for a few months. I was a housewife with a husband and three small children, but I had been a writer all my life and considered myself one. I had a newspaper column when I was very young and also had always written anything that fell my way to write. I saw no difference in writing the minutes of a PTA meeting, let us say, and writing prose fiction. It never even occurred to me to think I needed anyone to teach me how to write anything.

So why was I so excited by this? There I was, alone in my bedroom on a rainy afternoon and I read this in the paper and went crazy with excitement. It was a message to me, this notice in the paper. *It was about me.*

—⁓—

I left my children with the maid and got into my car and went to the library and took out all her books. I went home and read them. I think I read *The Wide Net* first, the book and the short story, and it is still my favorite book of hers and also my favorite story.

If my excitement had been high before, now it was at fever pitch.

It was still raining the next morning when I tore through the closets of my new house looking for things I had written. I collected ten of my newspaper columns, things I had written at Vanderbilt and I don't know what else. Poems, stories, anything that had been published anywhere. I was going to Millsaps to apply for Miss Welty's class but I was going as a *writer*, not a supplicant.

I do not know why I was so excited or why I still get excited thinking about it. I think I wanted to know another *writer*. I wanted to be in the presence of someone who also believed she was a *writer*, believed she had a right to that title, not because the world told her she did, but because she knew it to be true.

I was not disappointed. I marched into George Boyd's office (at the English department at Millsaps) and laid all my papers on his desk and said, you must let me in this class. He read for a few minutes, then he looked up and said, yes, you can be one of the chosen.

I found out later the class was already closed. He had taken a chance on me and stretched the rules, something he was not known for doing.

—⌘—

I was sent to the admissions office to apply to the school. I had been to four colleges before I got married and started having babies, and I think my transcripts were a mess. I either made an A in a subject or I dropped the class, but the grades from Vanderbilt were high. Anyway, they admitted me as a student and I signed up for other classes while I was there. I had a rich daddy, an indulgent mother, and help with the children. I could decide one afternoon to go back to school and it would be possible.

Then a few days went by and it was a Wednesday afternoon and I climbed the stairs to the second floor of the Millsaps Library and there she was, the divine Miss Welty, in all her humility and kindness and terrible strength and goodness and deep intelligence and generosity. I was in the presence of a *writer* and it was better than I had ever dreamed it could be.

ELLEN GILCHRIST

—⌘—

—⌘—

IX

One of Them was Dreaming

I first encountered a Eudora Welty story in a college course. The story was "Powerhouse." It interested but did not inspire me. The jazzy language was a neat trick, I thought—one I would try in my own writing some time—but then, in the 1980s, there were trendy, minimalist models. Besides, what could a gnomish, white woman possibly know about the life of a black musician? Perhaps she visited a Harlem nightclub in the 1930s and listened to the soulful swing of the Prez or the Lady, or Fats Waller, on whom "Powerhouse" is based. Perhaps the club was segregated, the musicians performing for an all-white audience that was slumming uptown and soon to return to the East Side where not one of the musicians dared set foot after dark lest he or she be followed by the police. Even Richard Wright, living in white-liberal Greenwich Village in the 1940s was shunned by his neighbors.

Then, I found out this writer was from Mississippi. I knew about Mississippi. It was the hardest place in America for black people. More black people lived there than any other state, and yet, they were the poorest, the most uneducated, and the most under-represented in the country. How dare this white Mississippian try to enter the aesthetic landscape of a black man. My mind snapped shut like a mousetrap, smushing that yellow cheese I called a brain.

A few years later, an instructor at a community college, I decided to teach a Welty story in a freshman class. Welty might not have been a choice at all, but by then I was living in the Deep South—Georgia—a place as dreaded in the mythology of my growing up as any prison camp, and I was becoming interested in the region. I remember the day I got the job, my grandmother had taken me aside and begged me not to go "down there." It was dangerous, she warned. I needed the work and I reasoned that I could make it a literary adventure like Jean Toomer had done. Toomer had grown up in Washington, D.C., the big city in my part of the world, and had taught in Sparta just fifty miles from where I was teaching. So with a somewhat indifferent attitude toward the literature of my new region, I read "Death of a Traveling Salesman," Welty's first published story.

Thinking as an English teacher, I was concerned about how I might compare this little story with Arthur Miller's great drama by a similar name. I read along with proper attention, following the ho-hum adventure of Mr. Bowman, the protagonist, when suddenly the language, the story, and how I viewed the avocation of the writer fell off a cliff. That cliff was not the one the shoe salesman Mr. Bowman drives off of at the beginning of the story; it was far more precipitous than that one. In the story, the characters are sitting in the firelight drinking moonshine, when the narrator observes casually: "The dogs slept; one of them was having a dream."

My imagination leapt. The pedant in me shriveled. Now, as if I were that pitiful shoe salesman trying to latch onto the enigmatic warmth of his hillbilly hosts, I began to see new possibilities in language and the role of the writer. This short, beautiful sentence came as a corruption of the literariness of the passage. Briefly it refocused my attention from the main characters to minor characters, from foreground to a detail of background, from humans to pets. Though a short declaration, what the sentence declared was extraordinary: These minor players, these hounds, had lives—not just lives—but dreams. This declaration broke open the egg of my imagination. Was it sloppy in its inconsistency of focus? Was it a corruption of point-of-view? *Whatever.* It was no less than a portal into the mystery of the story: The hillbilly dreams, the stupid wife dreams, the dog dreams—poor Mr. Shoe Salesman dreams and dreams haplessly. What's more, it was a portal into the mystery of writing. What else was fiction writing but dreaming out loud and bold?

In the Hemingway story, "The Short Happy Life of Francis Macomber," a story I was familiar with by the time I got to Welty, there is a similar disruption of point-of-view. A game hunter has shot a lion, and the narration switches its focus from the hunter to the hunted. The narrator tells the reader that the lion's flanks were "wet and hot," and that "his big yellow eyes narrowed with hate." A remarkable observation. Not only does it imply the animal's discomfort, but imbues the beast with emotion. Still in all of its reportorial exotica, Hemingway's passage did not, still does not, impress me as fundamentally as Welty's. The dog was *dreaming!* Much more than the instinctual life we generally ascribe to animals, much more than the emotional life Hemingway implied, Welty's dog had an *intuitive* life. He or she occupied not just the physical and emotional spaces, but also the universe of infinite possibilities.

—⁂—

I grew up in the country, in Virginia— Southern and Jim Crow, though by some degrees less harsh than Mississippi— or at least, my family thought so. As a child, I became acquainted with the night skies, particularly in the fall when the air was crisp and the most brilliant stars were out. With a cardboard telescope, I searched for gas clouds in Orion, and for the hazy Andromeda galaxy. On summer nights, I listened to the screech of cicadas and crickets, and the whistle of the whippoorwill. On

—⁂—

spring evenings, my search for tadpoles was guided by the croaks of frogs. In the winter, the whoo of a barn owl might break into my sleep. In the daytime, I watched the slow dancing of cumulus, often from the fanning branches at the top of a maple. The branches were a crow's nest from which I could survey the rolling farms and the blue ridges on the horizon. I had a dog, too. He was named Napoleon, but I called him Bean. He loved me, but I deserted him when I went off to the fast life of college.

Growing up close to nature, my greater interest was in science, not literature. I read science texts and science fiction, not great works. But rather than making me skeptical, my scientific interests led me to believe that the great pattern of existence—from big bang to seed germination—was mysterious. My Baptist and Pentecostal training had little influence on this perspective. I do not intend to mock religion by saying that *Star Trek* influenced me more. Nature was mysterious; it was the enigma that fueled my curiosity and creativity. Yet in all of my musings on the nature of things, I never once considered that a dog might dream until I read that line in Welty.

His breath rank with rabbit, his eyelids fluttering and his tail rapping the floor planks, what was that hound dreaming? Was he flushing quail—*run, little quail, run*? Or pressing his nose to a bitch's hind parts? Or was he dreaming of the stars? In his dream, did he sprout wings and fly off to join his kindred sky dogs, Major and Minor? Or did he dream of his master, his love for his master? Did he long for the firm stroke of his master's hand? Ahh, a man may become a wolf, but a dog is always a dog.

But why stop with the dreams of dogs? What of the stars? Do *they* dream? Do they dream of me, as I have dreamt of them and their faraway, dusty planets? Do they dream that I am setting down on one of those planets, with starlight, now sunlight, reflecting in parti-colored sparkles from the metal of my space-ship while creatures undreamed of creep along the crater's edge to greet me?

And the human dead? What will we dream? What memories? What regrets will spin in our hollow craniums? What joys and sorrows will churn beneath our yellow curves of ribs?

All of creation dreams, and sometimes these dreams mani-fest. This is the discovery that Welty foisted upon me.

—∞—

Though I have encountered her image in photographs and in film, I have never met Welty. I have never even been present at a reading or lecture she has given. I have been unlucky that way. Once a student of mine and his new bride, while on their hon-eymoon found themselves in Jackson, Mississippi. They had heard that Welty opened her house to visitors. They just hap-pened to have a copy of *Collected Stories* (they were English majors) and they dropped in on Welty to get the book signed. It took her a long time to come to the door and they thought she wouldn't answer, but just as they were about to turn away, the lock jangled and the door opened. She invited them in. She moved slowly. She told them to go ahead to the sitting room. She would catch up with them.

The sitting room was filled with stacks of magazines, newspapers, and letters. She said she tried to answer all her mail. She seemed genuinely interested in my student and his bride and they talked for half an hour. They didn't talk about literature, nor did Welty talk much about herself. She directed the conversation to subjects that made her guests feel easy. Welcomed. This is the kind of writer—no, the kind of *person*—I want to be. Open. Trusting. Generous.

—∿—

When I first saw Welty's book of photographs, *In Black and White,* I was not so generous. It was many years after I had been affected by the dreaming dog. In her work I saw pictures of black Mississippians of the 1930s and 1940s. One picture in particular struck at my core. It was a picture of a young woman dressed in a flapper's dress and hat; a fur coat was draped around her shoulders. She had a look of cheerful abandonment as if going off to a party. Perhaps her own birthday party. There was nothing undignified about the photograph—it was a rarely presented image of black southern life. Usually we are shown barefooted, ragged, and bent over cotton. Perhaps it was because the image cut against the grain that I reacted strongly to it. I had seen pictures like this in my grandmother's album, pictures of my great-aunts and cousins. Though I did not know the woman in the photo from Eve, I felt that my privacy, the privacy of my family, had been invaded. How dare this white woman take pictures of us and sell them for art? Again, I wanted to know what Welty knew about the lives of black people. In the South, blacks and whites have lived in the same space since the first slave was pushed from the ship at Jamestown, but whites, for the most part, have lived—and still do live—on top of us, not beside us, not with us. Traditionally, we have had to know them as a matter of survival, but they have not had the same necessity to know us intimately. When my mother did day work for Dr. and Mrs.—well, I won't name them—we all, Daddy and all the children, could tell you everything about that unnamed family. Which children were messy. Which were smart. Which were kind. Mrs. Unnamed often confided in my mother about Dr. Unnamed. But neither she nor her children knew much more about us than that we existed.

The writer, the artist, must be different. The writer tries to dream as others dream. The writer tries to know the other through dreams and tries to make sense of all the dreaming. Significantly, the writer knows that, though the variations are countless, we are dreaming the same dream whether we are black or white, human or dog. I squirm and bitch when I enter my own dream and the dream of my people through the eyes of a white dreamer; nonetheless, I have come to celebrate the dreaming. I celebrate the journey—whether into the powerhouse of black jazz or down a worn path through the pines. "Out of my way, all you foxes, owls, beetles, jack rabbits, coons and wild animals!"

Though Welty's pictures were in black and white, I believe she must have dreamt them in color. I do. Her pictures and her writing burst with color because they reach beyond the expectations of the average person—the somnambulant Dr. and Mrs. Unnamed—who seem never fully awake from or engrossed in their dreams. These unfortunates have no perspective on either their waking lives or their dreams, and yet, they have many Josephs to interpret for them: Seven fat cows and then seven lean cows—prepare for the famine! Instead, they believe in the dogma of the magis—a house in Green Acres with two cars in the garage and a TV in every room.

What would they dream if they would let themselves dream? Would they dream of angels on a ladder? Or of little black boys and black girls joining hands with little white boys and white girls? Or would they dream of rolling nine-pins in the woods with bearded, little men? Perhaps they would dream of walking down the Natchez Trace with Old Doc and his wide net, singing out loud as they walked together through "the changing-time."

"Any day now . . .," Doc says, "Hickory tree there will be yellow. Sweet-gum red, hickory yellow, dogwood red, sycamore yellow. . . . Magnolia and live-oak never die. Remember that. Persimmons will all get fit to eat, and the nuts will be dropping like rain all through the woods here. And run, little quail, run, for we'll be after you too."

ANTHONY GROOMS

—⚏—

X

For Ms. Welty at Ninety

I supposed I was surrounded by ignorant ghouls and ash-faced deacons as I grew a brain in Mississippi. I had heard the *oohs* and *ahs* about Miss Eudora, over there in my teenage-ripening town Jackson (beer, tobacco, jazz, blues, and midnight skank at the Dutch Bar), but I set them aside as the vaporings of schoolmarms desperate for any positive good in Mississippi, which was then essentially South Africa sealed in by a paper curtain of seg newspapers and the pastoral curtain of chant, *pro status quo*, from the pulpits. I was very Beat, trying badly to be an angel-headed hipster searching the night streets for an angry fix of howl, but with barely an urb—Jackson, simply wide and country—to do it in. I thought I knew all about the imagination, which, for one thing, could probably only happen in New York. (I'd been once to the Beatnik

Gaslight Café on McDougal in the Village and was still reeling from the cool—poets hollering over my coffee, big cup of grownup wayout depressed coffee, baby—but of course I knew only anger and the Big Pose.)

When I went up to writing school in Fayetteville, Arkansas, they were still talking about Eudora Welty, some of the hip dude brethren too, not just your local color culture vultures. So, also, I was deeply attuned, when one of my heroes, Henry Miller, was reported to have visited Ms. Welty to give his respects. Miller in *my* hometown, old grumpy mushmouthed *Jackson?* So I read "Powerhouse" and "Death of a Traveling Salesman" and found I knew little about the imagination. How could a *woman,* for God's sake, put the tune to such a jazzman and his nemesis, Uranus Knockwood? (Such was my male bias that I also read five stories by Flannery O'Connor and was raving about him, when somebody politely clued me in that the author was a woman. I was getting to be a bigger fool in school every day, which is maybe the point of a good school.) So I shut up and listened. "Death of a Traveling Salesman" was another act of soul-traveling magic— the way Welty was *in* the man here, his sick loneliness; the way the mule sticks its face in the window and looks at him; his sudden recognition the woman is pregnant and not old; the shock of his loss of love and simple communication, such as this country marriage represented! The metaphysical *inhabiting* of another soul, of another gender, and of such an alien order to herself, the artist. How could this be possible? My own father was an insurance salesman; I thought I knew the breed. Beyond mere empathy, or even "negative capability"—per Keats—these acts of art were simply genius. I had finally looked at genius straight-on, and it was frightening.

There was much work to be done, maybe *too* much, to be even a water boy on the team of this genius. So I scrapped it all, and feeling humble, began to write the first good stories of my life. I was not ashamed of my state's people anymore. I had not looked nearly deep enough. Ms. Welty taught me a lifelong lesson. Good things can come if you shut up, watch, and work. She dismissed from me the phony arrogance of the Beat stance and got me closer to a view of the intense life I had always sought in my younger scribblings.

I'll be thankful always for the extra life she made available to me and all of us.

BARRY HANNAH

—ɯɯ—

XI

The Essential Clue and Connection

I first read Eudora Welty after purchasing a remaindered textbook from a table at Kmart on the mere evidence of her indexed name. I do not know what year this was, but the textbook wore a little yellow sticker marked 78¢. I'd been on the lookout for Miss Welty ever since discovering her in *Bowen's Court*, dashing around Ireland with Elizabeth Bowen at the wheel. If Bowen liked her, that was good enough for me, so I risked my 78¢ and carried home a lot of pages which didn't matter (in mining, this is called "the overburden") and sifted out the pure ore: "A Worn Path."

I thought of my "discovery" as something Nicene: "True light of true light." Bowen from Woolf (think of them kneeling there that last visit, hemming the blackout curtains) and Welty ("Did you see that!") from Bowen as they flew along those dusty boreens.

Welty was a revelation and continues to be so. When I heard her voice on tape, reading Phoenix's story, I experienced a real shock, her voice sounds so much like my own mother's. The shock brought me to my senses. I recognized—in her human voice—that I had been hearing, had been dwelling among, had been living stories my whole life. I have no "anxiety of influence." She did not open *her* world to me; she opened *mine.*

I have never met Miss Welty, though I have tried to. That our paths have never crossed isn't the failure of our sojourn on this earth I once thought it was, nor a fate, nor a doom, for I have the habit of seeking her, and can always find her: before any new project, midway in a tangle (How do you cure a weak or disordered magnet? By placing it next to a strong one), and finally, in her Sabbath peace, when resting from my own work. I consult her *The Eye of the Story* as Romans studied auguries and New Agers their *I Ching.* I quote her. I hear her. I revere her. I forget and I remember her. I am always discovering her.

What I owe her, and what I will never forget, is that I saw and heard—from her first words—my own world, with kittens drinking raw milk from hubcaps, sixth graders singing "Paper of Pins," the convict catching the tossed pack of Marlboros from the drive-by stranger, the mailbox balloons shot with BBs, beautiful quick fools and the heartbreaking dead—my own world rendered visible. At that moment of first encounter, I "got it" the way Helen Keller got "water" at the pump—that essential clue and connection between thing and caption, making what I knew or only struggled to suspect worth conveying. Before I read Miss Welty, I thought I was a reader. After, I began to face facts and fiction, to develop what Miss Welty herself, writing about Phoenix, calls "the deep grained habit of love," which will, if anything can, take me as far as I need to go, and bring me home.

MARY HOOD

—⁘—

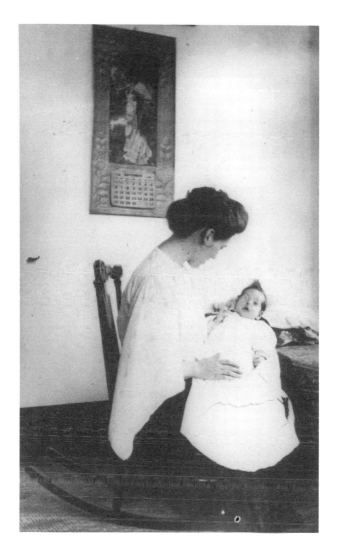

Mary Chestina Andrews Welty holding her daughter,
Eudora Alice Welty, June 1909, in Jackson, Mississippi.

Photograph courtesy of Eudora Welty Collection (EWC),
Mississippi Department of Archives and History (MDAH).

Eudora Welty's ninth birthday party, April 13, 1918, in Jackson. Left to right: Edward Welty, Jo Jeff Power, Jane Percy Slack, Bessie Smith, Sara Virginia Thompson, Eudora, Elizabeth Heidelberg, and Walter Welty.

Photograph courtesy of EWC, MDAH.

Welty at age thirteen, dressed for her piano recital, Jackson, 1922

Photograph courtesy of EWC, MDAH.

*Welty on the day of her graduation
from Central High School in Jackson, May 1925.*

Photograph courtesy of EWC, MDAH.

Welty in New Orleans, accompanying her father on a business trip to California, circa 1925.
Photograph courtesy of EWC, MDAH.

Welty with her ukelele in the early 1930s. According to Welty, "everyone played one."
Photograph courtesy of EWC, MDAH.

Welty and Hubert Creekmore at the Windsor Ruins, Port Gibson, Mississippi, 1954.

Photograph courtesy of Louis J. Lyell.

Frank Lyell and Welty in Austin, Texas, May 1963.

Photograph courtesy of Louis J. Lyell.

Welty Symposium, University of Mississippi, November 1977. Standing in front of a beauty salon in Oxford, Mississippi, from left to right, Karen Gilfoy, Jane Reid Petty, Welty, and Reynolds Price.

Photograph courtesy of Patti Carr Black.

Welty at home in Jackson,
enjoying bourbon and water, 1977.
Photograph courtesy of Patti Carr Black.

Welty and William Jay Smith
at Welty's seventy-fifth birthday party,
April 13, 1984, at Bill's Burger
House in Jackson.
Photograph courtesy of Patti Carr Black.

Queen Elizabeth 2   Photographed on board 1984

Trip to London, summer, 1984, on board the Queen Elizabeth 2. Standing
on deck, from left to right, Jane Reid Petty, Welty, and Patti Carr Black.
Photograph courtesy of Patti Carr Black.

Lunch at the Hotel Siena in Chapel Hill, 1988. From left to right, Louis D. Rubin, Jr.; Kaye Gibbons; Welty; Jill McCorkle; Lee Smith; Susan Ketchin; Clyde Edgerton; and Wyndham Robertson.

Photograph courtesy of Louis D. Rubin, Jr.

Fellowship of Southern Writers at the sixth biennial Conference on Southern Literature, Chattanooga, Tennessee, 1991. Seated, left to right, are Shelby Foote, Ellen Douglas; Welty; Cleanth Brooks, Andrew Lytle; Elizabeth Spencer; and Mary Lee Settle. Standing, left to right, are George Core; Fred Chappell; Peter Taylor; Wendell Berry; Louis D. Rubin, Jr.; James Dickey; Ernest J. Gaines; Romulus Linney; George Garrett; Walter Sullivan; Lewis Simpson; and C. Vann Woodward.

Photograph courtesy of Fellowship of Southern Writers Archives, University of Tennessee at Chattanooga.

*Welty and Richard Ford at the Mississippi Library Association
annual conference, November 1987.*

Photograph by Christine Wilson, courtesy of MDAH.

*Welty's eighty-fifth birthday celebration at Lemuria bookstore
in Jackson, April 1994. Pearl Amelia McHaney,
editor of this tribute volume, and Welty.*

Photograph by Michelle Stapleton, courtesy of the Jackson Clarion-Ledger.

XII

Why Welty Matters

*I*s it presumptuous for a Southern writer to claim he has been influenced by Eudora Welty?

Hardly. Rather it would seem the height of arrogance to suggest otherwise. Writing in the South, we are influenced by Welty in the same way we are all influenced by Shakespeare or Melville or Faulkner: Major writers alter our language, our idiom, shaping the writerly voices we claim to recognize as our own.

As an undergraduate, studying fiction writing seriously for the first time, I confess I paid little attention to Welty. The workshops I attended in the 1970s buzzed with excitement over the postmodernist experiments of Barth and Gass and Gardner, not the work of older writers we probably considered "conventional." I remember mentioning Katherine Anne Porter to a friend, who briefly made a face and insisted Porter wrote "for old ladies." My friend probably would have made the same comment about Welty, and at that time I might not have disagreed. Older now, at least marginally wiser, my friend and I likely would yield a limb to have written Porter's *Noon Wine*, or any of several stories in Welty's *A Curtain of Green*. "Petrified Man" and "Powerhouse" and "A Worn Path" and "Why I Live at the P.O." and the underappreciated, brilliant title story with its unexpected emotional wallop—how amazing, in retrospect, to understand that all these classics of the form were contained in Welty's first book, quietly published in 1941. Important, too, to understand that these stories—each so different from the other yet so technically brilliant, each linked to the rest in its clear-eyed moral vision and mastery of fictional voice—are also "experimental" in the deepest, most significant sense of that term. By contrast, it is now Gass, Gardner, and company who seem dated, their once-celebrated works fading from memory and disappearing from print. "They wrote for callow undergraduates," my friend might now remark.

Spanning this century, Welty's life has coincided with many trends, most of them forgotten or destined soon to be. Though her name long has been spoken with a respect bordering on reverence, I suspect that her artistic importance as a major Southern modernist remains insufficiently acknowledged, her short-story writer's boldness eclipsed by the larger-scale experiments of her fellow Mississippian and friendly colleague Faulkner. Welty herself surely has contributed to the aura of mildness and even gentility that clings to her reputation: her famous modesty and graciousness seem at odds with contemporary notions of the Important Writer as self indulgent or self-dramatizing, as ego-driven or victimized, as substance-abusing or suicidal. Do Important Writers live quietly in the same house for more than seventy years, answering the door to literary pilgrims who have the nerve to knock, and sometimes even inviting them inside for a chat?

In our culture, women authors have always created a persona, a social self, that seems to belie their status and achievement as artists. The Emily Dickinson assumed to be frail and "half-cracked," but who wrote some of the strongest and most subversive poems in English; the Flannery O'Connor who, as a docile Catholic, contacted her bishop for permission to read proscribed books, but whose own stories throbbed with rage and violence; the Sylvia Plath beneath whose 1950s good-girl exterior lurked a fierce mythological heroine who could eat men like air. Is it possible that Eudora Welty, the gracious Southern lady, concealed—and still conceals?—not only a sharp-witted satirist of regional manners but also an intrepid explorer of human mysteries no less profound than those evoked (and sometimes with greater sound and fury) by her Southern contemporaries? Such a point may seem obvious to longtime students of her work; but to the general public, Welty's carefully maintained exterior as a Yeatsian smiling public woman and her ongoing reputation as America's "most beloved writer" have served to obscure the quiet but unblinking ferocity of vision that gives her best work its extraordinary power.

It seems likely that most younger Southern writers look to the towering triad of Welty, Faulkner, and O'Connor not only for models of artistic craft and engagement. We also secure from them—especially as Southerners, and male writers no less than female—the permission to cross boundaries, to break whatever rules need to be broken in the pursuit of a personal vision. In 1941, Welty cannot have been unconcerned about how her first book of stories—innovative in technique and unapologetically bold in subject matter and theme—might be received by Southern readers, even by the small, presumably friendly, audience of family members and fellow writers. At this time, of course, Faulkner's reputation was in decline, his finest titles out of print; for most readers, Southern literature meant *Gone with the Wind*. And here came a soft-spoken, unmarried girl of thirty-three (for anyone unmarried and thirty-three in Jackson was still a girl) with a book of stories bristling with social criticism and taking on controversial issues of race and gender, a not particularly ladylike book about a boisterous, sensual, oversized black jazz musician ("Powerhouse"); about a group of women in a beauty parlor who, revealed in all their hypocritical and mean-spirited splendor, evoked moral sterility no less harshly than did Joyce's best stories about Dubliners ("Petrified Man"); about an aged black grandmother who encounters a lying, condescending white man and a cruel, condescending white woman ("A Worn

Path"); and about such assorted, non-genteel subjects as madness, suicide, and murder. According to Ann Waldron in her unauthorized biography of Welty, the young writer invited family members and friends to help her choose a title for this extraordinary first collection, and she must have witnessed more than a few raised eyebrows. In sardonic response, evidently, to her sympathetic treatment of black characters in the stories, Welty's brother suggested the title *Darkie Victory*.

Despite the sketchy quality of Waldron's biography, it does offer glimpses of a writer less saintly but perhaps more likable and certainly more human than the iconic image that springs to mind when we think Eudora Welty. It is inevitably refreshing, for instance, to read that Welty loathed another person: Carson McCullers.

But biographical considerations or academic assertions about Welty's contribution to literary modernism are finally less important to the practicing writer than the one thing that finally matters: her prose. Ah yes: her prose. Opening at random my much-thumbed copy of *The Collected Stories*, I come upon this sentence that brings Mrs. Larkin of "A Curtain of Green" to vivid life:

> *"Now the intense light like a tweezers picked out her clumsy, small figure in its old pair of men's overalls rolled up at the sleeves and trousers, separated it from the thick leaves, and made it look strange and yellow as she worked with a hoe——over-vigorous, disreputable, and heedless."*

Here is Phoenix Jackson in "A Worn Path," perpetrating the most delightful theft in American literature:

> "The deep lines in her face went into a fierce and different radiation. Without warning, she had seen with her own eyes a flashing nickel fall out of the man's pocket onto the ground. . . . The yellow palm of her hand came out from the fold of her apron. Her fingers slid down and along the ground under the piece of money with the grace and care they would have in lifting an egg from under a setting hen."

I can remember distinctly the moment when my mature appreciation of Welty began. A graduate student at Emory, I was about to fly home to Texas for a family visit and happened to see Eudora Welty herself in the Atlanta airport. A woman had stopped her, and from Welty's polite smiles, her modest ducking of her head, her repeated "Thank you, thank you so much," it was clear the woman was telling Welty how much she loved her work. I remember thinking the novelist probably had endured hundreds of such encounters, responding to each admirer with the same faultless courtesy. The next day, I visited a bookstore in Texas and bought several novels of Welty's I had not read. One of them was *Losing Battles*, which I showed my mother as we sat over coffee one morning. I had begun reading the novel and I pointed to the first paragraph. My mother read it to herself, then read it aloud slowly, enunciating the words with the cadenced deliberation they deserved:

"When the rooster crowed, the moon had still not left the world but was going down on flushed cheek, one day short of the full. A long thin cloud crossed it slowly, drawing itself out like a name being called. The air changed, as if a mile or so away a wooden door had swung open, and a smell, more of warmth than wet, from a river at low stage, moved upward into the clay hills that stood in darkness."

My mother paused, then put the book down and looked at me, blinking.

"Why, that's beautiful," she said.

And indeed it was.

GREG JOHNSON

—⚭—

XIII

Eudora Dear

Eudora dear:

I have been thinking how fortunate we were to have been born toward the end of the first decade of this century. To begin with, the quiet: except on the Fourth of July. No heavy trucks, no bulldozers, no power lawnmowers, no leaf blowers, no power saws. When there was a sound, just the clop-clop-cloppity-clop of a horse and buggy. You could count the automobiles. The grass was full of wonderful things—spring beauties, dandelions, the one-winged seeds of the maple trees, the shell of a locust that had made itself a new shell, sometimes a piece of tinfoil or a penny. There were shade trees everywhere and their branches met over the street. If there was a red light in the sky, you picked up the telephone receiver and asked Central where the fire was and she knew. Even when nobody's house was on fire, the fire horses had to be exercised and so sometimes on the way to school you got to see the fire engine. For music there was Schumann-Heink and Alma Gluck and Caruso and Scotti and Amelita Galli-Curci and John McCormack. Who could ask for more? The record player was called a Victrola and had to be wound before each record. The blossoms of the trumpet vine made very good orange gloves. In August the rising spirals of the locusts, in January the crunch of packed snow on the sidewalk and ice-landscapes on the windows when you woke up in the morning. Church bells on Sunday morning, wash lines on Monday. No air conditioning. On very hot nights you took your comforter and went from room to room until you found a doorway with a current of air and you lay down there and went to sleep. The streetcars in summer were open on the sides and you could get on or get off anywhere. At the end of the carline the conductor got out himself and reversed the overhead trolley. Palm leaf fans kept everybody cool. The sound of the ice-cream wagon could have come straight from fairyland. Ice cream made at home tasted of salt but was better than the boughten kind. When the man checked the overhead street lamps, he sometimes left a carbon stick behind where a child could find it and write his name with it. In August the katydids brought home the terrible truth that it was only six weeks more till frost. Sometimes it was, sometimes it wasn't. The same with when the groundhog saw his shadow. I saw William Jennings Bryan plain. On the platform of the Lincoln Chautauqua. You must have seen him too. He was everywhere. There were airplanes but nobody had actually seen one. Punk sticks and pennyroyal kept mosquitoes at a distance. If there was a light in an upstairs window after ten o'clock it meant that somebody was sick. The bobwhite and the whippoorwill were equally tireless. Before anybody was awake the milkman made his rounds, leaving the milk on the porch steps, in glass bottles, and the cream had already floated to the top of the bottle and was yellow. On Decoration Day old men in uniforms much too large for them who had fought in the Civil War, as some people prefer to say The War Between the States, led the parade. The flag had forty-eight stars and thirteen stripes. There were so many Oz books at the library that you could never come to the end of them (only some were always out). George Washington's birthday was celebrated on the actual day, though the day he cut down the cherry tree nobody has ever announced that I know of. It cost 3¢ to mail a letter, or was it 2¢? Everybody knew the name of everybody else's horse and dog, and there was no extra charge for the rainbow.

Even more fortunate was the fact that we knew each other and were friends.

With love on your ninetieth from
Emmy, Kate, Brookie, and Bill Maxwell

WILLIAM MAXWELL

—∿—

XIV

Paradise Road

My connections with Eudora go back considerably. I was born in a house two blocks from hers in the Belhaven neighborhood of Jackson. I was christened in the church of her childhood, the Galloway Memorial Methodist Church, where as a girl she took her nickel to Sunday school in her glove, and when it was time to take up collection, she would pull the nickel out damp with sweat. She knew my mother, my grandparents, and my eccentric spinster great-aunts Maggie and Susie Harper. I first met her when I was eight or nine years old. She always shopped for groceries at an erstwhile establishment called the Jitney Jungle with wooden floors and flypaper dangling from the ceilings. My great-aunts used the Jitney as their "pantry," Eudora would remind me years later. One afternoon during World War II, on one of my many sojourns in Jackson from Yazoo City, I went with Aunt Maggie in her flowing black dress so she could fetch a head of lettuce, or a muskmelon perhaps, but mainly to hear the gossip from the other ladies of the Belhaven vicinity. Eudora was at the vegetable counter when Aunt Maggie introduced us. I remember she was tall and slender, and the luminous blue eyes. As we were leaving my great-aunt whispered to me, "She writes those stories her *own* self."

I once said to her years later that I read "A Worn Path" in the seventh grade, and it made me want to be a writer someday. "I'm so glad," she said.

One recent Sunday my wife JoAnne and I drove Eudora along the dirt and gravel back roads of Yazoo County, Mississippi, some forty miles north of Jackson. The spooky kudzu-enveloped terrain could have been right out of her fiction. Like a child dwarfed by the stark bluffs outside the car window, she rode shotgun through the sunlight and misty shadows. "I haven't seen another car yet," she noted at one point. "When was the last time we saw a human being?"

At the crest of a bosky hill, a narrower and darker byway intersected with the one on which we were traveling. "Eudora, I'm going to make a left and drive down Paradise Road," I said.

"We'd be fools if we didn't," she replied.

WILLIE MORRIS

—᠗—

XV

Golden Apples

I left the books by Eudora Welty on their shelf and sat down to discover what bits of the stories would surface in my mind from all those pages I had read and reread. And so many things came crowding in, from the warm caramel cake in Lily Daw's lap to the screams of Gabriela on the boat to Naples, that I had to settle on one book, which happened to be the first book of hers that I ever read and the one that has turned out to be my final favorite. *The Golden Apples.* Here are some things seen out of the corner of the eye, that will probably stay with me forever:

—*Missie Spights fastening her corset behind the kitchen door, in the house where Miss Rainey lies dead. . . . No. That's Missie Spights Littlejohn. She's married, she married from off.*

—Parnell Moody in the same kitchen drying every circle of the potato masher, with such care.

—In another house—the Starks'—Maideen who will kill herself (Old Man Moody of the Seed and Feed running out into the street with her in his arms) is saying, "I look too tacky and mussed when I work in the store all day to be coming in anybody's strange house."

"You're by far the freshest one here, my dear," says Miss Lizzie Stark. ("You men. You got us beat in the end," says Miss Lizzie on another occasion, interrupting her own account of a bridge game. "We'd know you through and through except we never know what ails you.")

—Virgie Rainey on a wet day at recess in the school basement threatening to beat her brains out against the wall ("Beat them out, then," says the teacher.) And drinking vanilla out of the bottle. And playing Für Elis on the picture show piano, while the blue and gold advertisement for the Morgana Bugle shivers on the screen.

—Virgie Rainey naked in the warm water of the Big Black River in the middle of a summer night. The same Black River in which Mr. Sissum drowned and King MacLain didn't, though they dragged it nine miles down for Miss Snowdie's sake.

—The Starks' electric car rocking over the landscape like an upright piano.

—And Loch's mother, glimmering in the dark at the foot of his bed after a momentous day, saying—with little waits in her voice—"Listen, and I'll tell you what Miss Nell served at the party. . . . A cup made out of toast, filled with creamed chicken, fairly warm. . . ."

I have to stop, even before I get to the cut-out jack-o'-lanterns on the schoolhouse windows when King MacLain first come courting Miss Snowdie, or the long switch of yellow hair in Kate Rainey's trunk. Her mother's young yellow hair, that Virgie never saw while it still matched.

I stop not just because there's so much coming back to me, but because I am overwhelmed with a terrible longing. Stabbed to the heart, as Miss Kate Rainey or perhaps Miss Perdita Mayo would say, by the changes, the losses in our lives. By the beauty of our lives streaming by, in Morgana and elsewhere.

That is my feeling as a reader. The writer's feeling, just as sharp, is a double one. Gratitude and amazed delight. And utter discouragement. Writing can be this good, it's been done. Something has been proved here, no use now trying to prove it again.

The first copy of *The Golden Apples* that I read was one I got from the West Vancouver Public Library, sometime in the mid-fifties. I remember the quote on the cover, though I don't remember who had provided it. "She writes exquisitely, she creates a world." Even at the time, the word "exquisitely" faintly disturbed me. As if it meant less now, than when it was put down, having gone a little pale and wispy, bringing to mind a frill of fine lace. So I put that aside, thinking that what I found in the book must never be mistaken for decoration. But "creates a world"—that was more like it. And it didn't mean—it doesn't mean—simply to set out the right furniture and catch the exact shades of speech and put the right food on the table and the right concerns in people's heads—so true, as we say, to life. More than skill must be involved, more than a sharp eye and a quick ear. The story must be imagined so deeply and devoutly that everything in it seems to bloom of its own accord and to be connected, then, to our own lives which suddenly, as we read, take on a hard beauty, a familiar strangeness, the importance of a dream which can't be disputed or explained. Everything is telling you, Stop. Hold on. Here it is. Here too. Remember.

Gratitude seems paltry and amazement is somehow beside the point. You must just say yes, that's it, that's what's been here, all the time.

ALICE MUNRO

XVI

On My First Becoming Acquainted with Eudora Welty and Her Work

This is really a love affair, and how can one write about such things without feeling at once shy and eager? For I will try to explain why my reading Eudora Welty's work and meeting her later and knowing her has been the passion of my life, something of the heart, and something of the soul after being first something of the mind.

That early fall of 1968 will forever remain a luminous memory. Faint traces of chill were already on the air, but they could not alter the bright exhilarating atmosphere of a Virginia fall. With our two young children, we had just arrived from Burgundy, my husband to work on the William Faulkner collections and the four of us already hoping to stay for two years in that South whose many-faceted history, legends, and literature had fed our imaginations for years. In my own case, I was given the great gift of time and felt free to explore life at and around the University of Virginia, above all, at thirty, with the Agrégation behind me and a leave of absence before me, I felt free to read all I wanted. Charlottesville was a small town after Lyon and Paris where I had grown up, but it was brimming with intellectual and artistic activity. We had just lived through the challenge of May 1968, and its epoch-making spirit of questioning, reappraising, of reversal and creativity, a time of exalted high spirits and freedom. In a word, we were prepared for the great revolutions of the mind and eager to think differently.

I will never forget that evening and the room in the lovely small house we rented for two years, a stone's throw away from the "Grounds," in a slowly decaying neighborhood of charming old ladies, whose ancestry was as irreproachable as their kindness to us. I had not been prepared for this, as they gave me keys to understanding a certain South and taught me much to appraise the background of Welty's fiction. And on that evening that was to change my life, I read one after the other the seventeen stories of *A Curtain of Green*, which my husband had just given me saying: "You may like this. Eudora Welty gave a reading in Charlottesville a few months ago, and is highly thought of here. Michel Gresset is translating one of the stories for *La Nouvelle Revue Française.*"

What struck me at the time and was to enthrall me forever was the tone of the stories, which showed remarkable strength and mastery in the fusing of the ordinary into the extraordinary, by which I mean making the invisible visible and offering glimpses into the continent of secret lives and the real, something that avant-garde painting had been trying to capture for years, but which was very new in literature. In spite of their variety in mood, theme, wit and humor, there was a *marque de fabrique* that unmistakably branded their author as a great writer. Such mastery in the craft of storytelling I had seldom met, except with Balzac, Julien Gracq, perhaps, or Albert Camus, for I had not yet read the short stories of Virginia Woolf or Karen Blixen. At the same time, I felt that the new American short story writers, mostly male, were not so new after all, for here were the seeds of their craft. Most intriguing, as well as captivating, was the sensuousness of Welty's texts, and the way they enlarged and estranged the world. When I closed the book, I felt as if I had been invited to explore a strange new land so close to, yet so remote from, the world short fiction usually presents. Most exhilarating for me, almost fever-giving, was the newly awakened sense that here was truth about life, the kind of aesthetic and spiritual truth that scorns conventions and twists expected plots. The stories resisted a first reading too, and that was not their least charm. Of "A Memory," for instance, as sharer of such experiences, I liked the first love atmosphere with its delicate day dreaming, the violent scenes on the beach, and I acknowledged the technique of the embedded memories. Yet, I felt that the gist of the story had eluded me, that I must read it and read it again and again. Today, I know how true this is of all Welty's stories, no matter how short or simple they seem to be, and how endless is the task of interpreting them. The proof of their excellence lies in their providing fresh surprise at every new reading.

Later that first night, after experiencing something like an illumination, I decided I would try to probe their secrets and grasp their mysteries, not with the fear of destroying their beauty, but with the hope of bringing it to light through a better understanding. I felt seized by a rage or a hope, which is every critic's hope, and every lover's hope, that my passion would be shared by others. The few critical books and essays I could find soon convinced me that there was ample room for new critical approaches. I had a whole new school to choose from at home with Barthes, Derrida, René Girard or Georges Poulet, among them, together with Foucault or Baudrillard.

So I set to work, yet, I had not met Miss Welty. In the summer of 1972, during another trip to the United States, I wrote to ask Miss Welty if I could call on her in Jackson. In a gesture so typical of her desire to respect her engagements, and to protect herself and her work from the interruptions of unknown visitors, she graciously answered that she was working "on a project that involved others" and regretted to have to decline the interview. In fact, she was writing her superb essay "Some Notes on Time in Fiction," which came out in the first Eudora Welty issue of the *Mississippi Quarterly*, Fall 1973. I was to wait five more years.

The occasion was superb: the inauguration on November 10–12, 1977, of the Center for the Study of Southern Culture at the University of Mississippi. Bill Ferris, its new director, had asked Professor Louis Dollarhide to organize a symposium honoring Eudora Welty, "Mississippi's greatest living author." On the panel were seven speakers, chosen out of a spirit of celebration and friendship; all except one were fellow Mississippians. There were critics who had launched Eudora Welty into the world of literature by publishing her first short stories, like Cleanth Brooks, writers who had found themselves and learned their craft under her teaching creative writing, like Reynolds Price, or long-time friends like the poet William Jay Smith or Mississippi historian Charlotte Capers. All were famous and had left their marks in the literary world. There were also younger scholars like Michael Kreyling, Peggy W. Prenshaw, and Noel Polk, who too would soon leave their marks in the critical world. The symposium had attracted many scholars from the South, and two Europeans in love with Eudora Welty's work, Jan Nordby Gretlund from Denmark and myself from France. Those three glorious days in Oxford, when the old trees of the campus were in their last autumn magnificence have left indelible memories. The great excitement was the presence of Eudora Welty herself, smiling and gracious, if a little reserved, taking in everything with her penetrating eye and moved by so much love and heartfelt admiration. There were wonderful parties too, elegant and friendly in that inimitable Southern manner. For me, it was where I met a number of Welty scholars who were to become friends over the years, and, most important, where I briefly met Eudora Welty with the promise to visit her in Jackson in January 1978.

From the beginning of our acquaintance, in that subtle way of hers, Eudora Welty has proved most kind and appreciative, and always in control. She can be the warmest and most generous hostess, as well as open to informal discussions of her work and that of others. Her great intelligence, her vast culture, and her alertness to all that is new, exciting, and innovative in the world of art and literature fill her conversation with brilliance and wit. With a larger audience and visitors with whom she shares a lifelong complicity, the conversation becomes an art, and reaches peaks of laughter and humor. Storytelling is then at its best, as I have been an occasional, happy listener. When I first saw her living room, crowded with new books by both established authors and young new ones, I felt that this was an expansion of her ever curious mind and of her exquisite heart. When appreciative of an artist, Eudora Welty is warm in her praise, as she was on that afternoon when she directed me towards a comfortable chair close to a small table with piles of new books, and among them *Rock Springs* by Richard Ford. The book had just come out and she was very eulogistic, inviting me to read it straightaway.

After that cold January 1978, when she was so very kind to me, I felt truly comforted in my admiration. The human being behind the artist had an all-encompassing width and depth; now, I told myself, I can begin to see where such clear vision of life comes from. It was after that other glorious celebration of her talent on the occasion of her seventy-fifth anniversary, organized by Professor Austin Wilson on April 13, 1984, in Jackson, when all kinds of artists so deeply responded to her charisma, that I felt that I would always be a welcome visitor at her home. And for fifteen years this has been true, as true friendship grew between us. The awe which all great artists inspire is still here, but somewhat mellowed by love.

The study of Eudora Welty's fiction has been my continuing work, the key that critically opened other fictions to me. Critical fashions come and go, but I remain convinced that the great gift of Eudora Welty to writers in this twentieth century is her passion for the art of storytelling. Through her own stories and her critical essays she has taught at least two generations of writers. Without her, the art of fiction would not have reached such splendid developments, for like the few truly great writers in this century, she has inspired artists all over the world as she has helped readers from all over the world to live better and deeper.

Above all, what marks Eudora Welty as a dominant figure in twentieth-century American literature, is the way she has pursued her examination of illusions and delusions, prejudice and violence. Renewing the innovative aesthetic gesture of the painters who influenced her vision and technique in her youth, *she writes the ground as figure*—less about the South than with the South. The South then becomes the very substance with which she probes burning and ever-present issues: racism, gender, politics. This is why her photographs of defiant heroic African-American women must be construed as self-portraits, and her fictionalizing black and white men and women, as emblems of the interpenetrating horror and greatness of the Human Condition.

DANIÈLE PITAVY-SOUQUES

—ɯ—

XVII

Finding Eudora

I first encountered Eudora Welty's name and a piece of her work when I was a high school freshman in Raleigh in 1947–48. Her story "A Worn Path" was printed in our literature textbook (the name of which I've long since forgot). I know that, along with my colleagues in the class, I read the story; and we must have discussed it with our young teacher Mary Barber. Oddly, what I remember most clearly about that early encounter is not the great story itself and its resemblance to an old black woman of my own acquaintance but the illustration which the textbook provided—old Aunt Phoenix Jackson bent nearly double to recover a single nickel from the ground. I had watched more than one such moment myself in what amounted to the late days of slavery in a Carolina county more than two-thirds black.

While my own ambition to write had declared itself a year earlier, in the self-entrapment of adolescence, I was a good distance off from being concerned with the work accomplished around me in my part of America. I'd already read, and liked, Faulkner's "A Rose for Emily," for instance, but had felt no eagerness to pursue his other work. And the same was true of Welty. In fact, it would be the better part of a decade before I felt compelled to read more of her work. That was during my senior year at Duke University, in a narrative-writing course taught by the famous William Blackburn. Blackburn knew that Welty was coming to campus in February 1955 to present a lecture, and he asked the members of his writing class to read the recently issued Modern Library edition of her *Selected Stories.* Then, piece by piece, we'd discuss the work in our afternoon meetings.

—⋙—

As I began that reading, I was on the verge of my twenty-second birthday. My professional ambitions were higher than ever, I'd written one brief story that Blackburn called simply "professional," and I was casting round for new subject matter to see me through the semester's work. More than I knew then, I was poised for discovering that the world of Welty's early fiction resembled closely the world of my own childhood and youth, both in physical detail and emotional substance. The discovery was much like the sudden finding, in a new town or place, of a friend who seems to have been yours forever.

Such a discovery might well have been devastating—like discovering, once you've finished your doctoral dissertation, that a suspiciously similar study has just been published. From the start of my relations with Welty's fiction, though, I could see that there were decisive differences of tone and focus between her sense of the world and the one of which I'd been increasingly conscious since adolescence. I shared, for instance, her sense of the hilarity of much in our mutual circles and of the centrality of African-Americans in our midst; but I knew at once that our responses to such matters were (given our ages and the geographical shadings of our native places) inevitably divergent and therefore liberating for me. I could admire and even love her achievement and never feel a trace of envy.

—m—

It took me a year or so—by which time I was a graduate student in England, and Welty and I had become friends—to understand that a reality even larger than a related set of subjects bound us. And now, more than forty years later, those ramified subjects bind us still in our work and our friendship.

It may best be described as a kind of addicting joy in having such unbounded worlds to watch, both old and young, and to remake as long as human strength allows.

REYNOLDS PRICE

XVIII

Things from Out in the World

"Time goes like a dream no matter how hard you run, and all the time we heard things from out in the world that we listened to but that still didn't mean we believed them."

—"Shower of Gold," *The Golden Apples*

*J*n the summer of 1949 I was twenty-five years old, a would-be writer working at a boring job on a newspaper copydesk in Wilmington, Delaware. My favorite writer, the one I thought I wished to emulate, was Thomas Wolfe. What I identified with was the romantic egocentricity, the "O Lost!" motif: "A Legend of Man's Hunger in His Youth." "He twisted his throat with a wild cry."

In the *New Yorker* I read a review by Hamilton Basso of a book entitled *The Golden Apples*. It prompted me to read the book. *The*

Golden Apples consisted of a set of related stories, all but one of them located in a town in Mississippi. What the various characters did and said was for the most part neither exceptional nor world-shaking. The events were such as might happen in any Southern town or small city. It ended with a funeral and then a middle-aged woman sitting under a tree and watching the rain: "October rain on Mississippi fields. The rain of fall, maybe on the whole South, for all she knew on the everywhere. She stared into its magnitude."

There was something about the stories that made them more than just a group of stories. Lurking with the seemingly mundane surface doings, things were going on. Within the apparently commonplace happenings among unexceptional people—*part of* those happenings, causing those people to turn out to be not unexceptional but extraordinary—important and remarkable perceptions about what human experience was about were revealing themselves.

I could not set the book aside. I kept coming back to it. That winter, back in Baltimore at Johns Hopkins, I was prompted to write a review of it and several other books by Southern authors for *The Hopkins Review.* It was not a very discerning review; the best I can say for it is that it did convey the idea that there was that about *The Golden Apples* that lifted it out of the commonplace and made it memorable.

In Thomas Wolfe everything had seemed powerful and obvious. In Eudora Welty there was mystery in the prose. The art did not advertise itself; it was the kind of artistry that concealed art. You had to look for the secrets, the equivocations, the meanings about people, just as you did in real life. It made me keep thinking and wondering. Why did Cassie Morrison recall that poem in her dreams? What was the poem? What kind of flower was it that the old woman left at Virgie Rainey's house late at night after Virgie's mother died? Why, when Virgie had returned to Morgana after trying to live elsewhere, had there been a thunderclap? Why did Jinny Love Stark insist so desperately upon waving the towel while the Boy Scout Loch Morrison worked to resuscitate the drowned orphan girl's life? Why, when Mr. Sissum was being buried, did the old music teacher Miss Eckhardt keep nodding her head back and forth? All such things were in themselves natural; but why did they stand out so in retrospect? *Why?*

I could not forget those stories, and did not want to. Their artistry grew on me; they were luminous. Through them—in them—I learned how fiction worked from *within.* I discovered a critical vocation.

LOUIS D. RUBIN, JR.

—∭—

XIX

Marble Cake

*I*t was the spring semester of my sophomore year, 1966. The old brick buildings and long green lawns of Hollins College in Roanoke, Virginia, were festooned with blooming dogwoods and daffodils and redbuds—or maybe those redbuds were what we called sarvis in the mountains back home, in far southwest Virginia, where I came from. Where I came from but was determined to leave, totally and henceforth, in my quest to *be a writer*. Although I was beginning to have my doubts, since I was not doing so well, so far, in my writing classes at Hollins, receiving B's and C's and cryptic little comments from Lex Allen and Richard Dillard which said, basically, "Write what you know." I thought this was terrible advice; I didn't know what I knew. All I knew was that I was certainly not going to write anything about Grundy, Viriginia, ever, that was for sure. My last glimpse of home had been my mother and my two aunts sitting on the porch drinking iced tea and talking (endlessly) about whether one of my aunts did or did not have colitis. Well! I was outta there!

But I was still drunk on words and books, just as I had been as a child, when I used to read under the covers with a flashlight all night long. My favorite professor was Louis D. Rubin, who was introducing us to Southern literature; I hadn't even known it existed when we started out. I had already gotten drunk on Faulkner a couple of times, then had to go to the infirmary for a whole day when we read William Styron's *Lie Down in Darkness*— I got so "wrought up," as my mother used to say. She didn't hold with too much reading as a general rule, for this very reason.

Even so, I considered cutting class on the day that this woman with the funny name, from Mississippi, was coming to visit us. She was on campus, I believe, to receive the Hollins Medal, undoubtedly engineered by Louis D. Rubin, one of her earliest and greatest champions. But *I* had never heard of her, and it was so pretty outside, a great day to cut class and go up to Carvin's Cove and drink some beer or just stomp moodily around campus smoking cigarettes and acting like a writer . . . this was my plan until I ran into Mr. Rubin in the campus post office, and then I *had* to go to class.

But the minute I walked into the room, I realized that something special was going to happen. For one thing, there were a *lot more people* in that old high-ceilinged classroom than we had ever had there before, and for another thing, some of them were *male,* a rarity at Hollins in those days. The seats in the back of the room were filling up fast with faculty from our own college and from other area colleges too (beards, leather patches on the elbows of their ratty sports jackets: *not your dad)* as well as graduate students from UVA and W&L. The graduate students needed haircuts and looked intense. In fact, they looked exactly like the fabled Sixties, reputed to be happening somewhere outside our fairytale Blue Ridge campus at that very time.

A ripple of anticipation ran through the crowd. Mr. Rubin was ushering Eudora Welty into the room.

I was deeply disappointed. Why, she certainly didn't look like a writer! She didn't have a cape, or boots, or anything. What she wore was one of those nice-lady print voile dresses that buttoned up the front, just like all the other nice ladies I had known all my life, just like my mother and all her friends. In fact, she looked a little bit like Miss Nellie Hart, my eighth grade English teacher. (My favorite English teacher ever, but *still....*) I lost interest immediately.

I can't remember what Mr. Rubin said when he introduced her; I was probably too busy stealing glances into the back of the room while appearing *not* to.

Then, suddenly, Eudora Welty was reading "A Worn Path" out loud in her fast, light voice that seemed to sing along with the words of the story. And I was *right there*—in Mississippi with Phoenix Jackson as she sets out to get the medicine for her grandson, encountering the thorny bush, the scarecrow, and the black dog, the young hunter, and the lady along the way. I could see that "pearly cloud of mistletoe" near the beginning and then Phoenix's little grandson near the end: "He got a sweet look. He going to last. He wear a little patch quilt and peep out holding his mouth open like a little bird." I sat stunned when it was over.

Miss Welty had seemed perfectly composed as she was reading; her face was luminous, lit from within. Now, having finished, she looked nearly shy, though her huge blue eyes were shining. "Well," she said, looking all around, "any questions?" Hands waved everywhere.

She chose the young man who seemed the most impassioned. Knowing what I know now, I'll bet his dissertation was riding on his question. He leapt to his feet to ask it.

"I wonder," he said, his dark curly hair going everywhere, "if you could comment upon your choice of marble cake as a symbol of the fusion between dream and reality, between the temporal and the eternal, the union of yin and yang. . . ." He made yin-yang motions with his hands.

Miss Welty smiled sweetly at him. "Well," she said slowly, considering, "it's a lovely cake, and it's a recipe that has been in my family for years."

It would be years before I would understand that exchange, what really took place in our classroom that day. Later, in the final section of *One Writer's Beginnings*, Miss Welty would put it best when she wrote that "the outside world is the vital component of my inner life. My work, in the terms in which I see it, is as dearly matched to the world as its secret sharer. My imagination takes its strength and guides its direction from what I see and hear and learn and feel and remember of my living world."

My immediate response to Miss Welty's visit was to read everything she had ever written, of course. And it was like that proverbial lightbulb clicked on in my head—suddenly, I knew what I knew! With the awful arrogance of the nineteen-year-old, I decided that Eudora Welty hadn't been anywhere much either, and yet she wrote the best stories I had ever read. I sat down and wrote a little story myself, about three mountain women sitting on a porch drinking iced tea and talking endlessly about whether one of them does or does not have colitis. I got an A on it.

LEE SMITH

—⚮—

XX

The Listener

This tribute, written for Eudora Welty's seventy-fifth birthday, is now reprinted for her ninetieth. The Haitian painting mentioned in the final stanza is a present I made to her and I like to think that in its depiction of an exquisite and unique fragility it somehow symbolizes the friendship that I value so greatly. I hope that she will look at it again on April 13, 1999 and think of all the joyous times we have spent together since we first met fifty years ago.

—W. J. S.

I

One day when you sat in a ring in a kindergarten class to draw
three daffodils,

you found that while you drew, your freshly sharpened pencil and
the cup of the yellow daffodil

gave off the same whiff, and you thought it natural that the
pencil, drawing,

should have the same smell as the flower drawn—part, as it
should be, of the art lesson—

for children like animals use all their senses to discover the
world, and then the artist

comes along to discover it again (but there are some like you who
have never lost the child's world,

whose works are filled with all they have seen, touched, tasted,
and smelled, and especially

with all they have heard)—and you were, first of all, a listener.

Taken out of school when you were six years old and put to bed
because of a "fast-beating heart,"

you covered your skin with transfer pictures of roses, flags,
battleships and rattlesnakes,

and kept up with your class at the Jefferson Davis Grammar School
    across the street from the window at your side,

listening for Miss Duling's brass bell and watching the children
    eat at recess (you *knew* their sandwiches),

and when your parents draped the lampshade beside you with a sheet
    of the daily paper tilted like a hat brim

and sat in the lighted part of the room talking, you listened
    to every word,

too young to know what to listen *for,* but happy in the presence of
    the great secret, of their just being there together,

that secret and your fast-beating heart in step together, their
    faces in the cone of yellow light

under the newspaper shade with its brown pear-shaped scorch where
    it had once overheated,

and so early on you became the "privileged observer," the "loving
    kind," getting your distance as

you did later for photographs—frame, proportion, perspective,
    the values of light and shade

all determined by the distance of the observing eye—(and beginning
    to write, drawing slowly

close to people, noting and guessing, apprehending, hoping, drawing
your eventual conclusions from your own heart,

and then when time and imagination led you on, plunging ahead); and
back in school, you listened

to the sober accretion of a Latin sentence, real, intact, and built
to stay like the Mississippi

State Capitol at the top of your street, which you could walk through
on the way

to school and hear underfoot your echo on its marble floor, and, over
you, the bell of its rotunda;

listened in the Carnegie Library ("through the Capitol" was the
way to the Library),

with SILENCE in big black letters tacked up everywhere, to Mrs.
Calloway's commanding voice

above the seething sound of her electric fan turned on her streaming
face as she told you

that only two books could be checked out at a time and no book could
be returned

the same day it was borrowed, and you took your two home in your
bicycle basket, your only fear

that the books would end too soon; listened at Sunday School in
taffeta dress and hot, white gloves,

the elastic of your Madge Evans hat cutting under your chin, while
Miss Hattie kept time next to the piano,

with both arms, one clutching a broken chair leg, beating the air
with chopping motions, her voice

rising above the others: "Bring them in! Bring them in! Bring them
in from the fields of sin!

Bring the little ones to Jesus!" And listened, after Sunday School
when you went to visit

your father's insurance office, with nobody else in the building,
and even the water

in the cooler dead quiet, warm and flat, listened on his dictaphone
(the first in Jackson)

to his voice addressing his secretary, who always wore her hair in
stylish puffs

over her ears (and you had seen her with the earphones on top of
the puffs); and

in West Virginia, after the strumming of the long-necked banjos of
Uncle Mose and Uncle Carl,

listened to the mountain silence until you could hear as far into
it as the faintest clink of a cowbell.

II

Today you sit at your typewriter at the top of the stairs in the
quiet house where the clocks answer

one another as they did in your childhood, and there at the
confluence

of your inner and outer lives, the stories come to the tips of
your fingers while you listen

for them still: and then of a sudden the pigeons rush out of
the eaves, their wings

clattering against your window, and frightened as you were long
ago by your grandmother's pigeons,

your fingers skim over the keys, but now you know that the pigeons
are simply demanding their own story

as they once did, and that story is love, and they receive it thus—
LOVVVVVVVVVVVVVVVVVVVVE—on the keys,

and, as the pages pile up at your side, to keep the flow of the
story clear, you rise

and pin them together top to bottom just as Fannie, the black
  seamstress, used to pin

your dresses on you while you strained to hear the stories she had
  brought from all over town.

Now on your birthday we ask you to come down the stairs, trailing
  that train of stories,

that long lustrous ribbon of fiction to tie up a present for the
  world from its privileged observer,

come down to the couch beneath that primitive painting in which
  bird's eggs rest out on a limb

against a background of delicate robin's-egg blue, and we will
  gather at your feet

while you read to us in the deliberate rhythms of the old woman
  making her way down the worn path

and in the loony lickety-split lilt of the little girl locked
  up in the PO,

and in the rip-roaring rocking rhythms of Edna Earle as she ponders
  the Ponder heart,

come down and tell us again all those tales dredged up from the
  Delta, the piney woods, and the black bayous,

all as shining in your words as the blue Milk of Magnesia bottles
   on old Solomon's prize bottle tree;

and the dark outside the window will be dark as it once was dark,
   and the lightning bugs will rise

and signal through the branches of the sycamore, and the moon
   will climb,

and we will listen, as you have taught us to listen—in debt
   to you until the end of time.

WILLIAM JAY SMITH

XXI

For the Ninetieth

To have been friends with anybody for an unbroken fifty-six years is a phenomenon worth mention. But for two writers to be friends for that long surely belongs in the *Guinness Book of Records*. Between sensitive souls, so much can go astray—hurt feelings, adverse criticism, chance remarks repeated. The list is long. Though Eudora is an outspoken woman, when occasion demands, and is hardly the sweet and gentle lady some like to believe she is, her sensitivity takes the form of feeling *for* the other person. She can guess what is going on in that other mind and heart, and mainly she can respect it also, a rare trait. It can guarantee a long friendship, and she has nurtured many of those.

I first met Eudora Welty when I was a student at Belhaven College, at that time a small Presbyterian girls' school bordered on one side by Pinehurst Street where, in 1942, lived a young woman who had just published a collection of stories titled *A Curtain of Green*. We invited her to come to our creative writing group, a bunch of girlish amateurs who nonetheless liked to think we valued real writing even if we could not yet claim to produce it.

She came and listened politely to our efforts, and when later I walked back across the campus with her and we began to talk and laugh, talk and laugh, I had the first face-to-face experience of the magic that saturates her writing.

I try to choose which of the many times we met later that I find most joyous to recall. Was it when we were staying in New York in the same hotel in 1952? She was being inducted into the American Academy. I was receiving a prize there as well. We stayed on a few days and used to call each other between floors to meet for drinks in the hotel bar, or to go to a play or a movie. Some of her Jackson acquaintances had jobs in New York. One lived down near the village, and we would meet at her apartment for drinks and troop out across Washington Square to the Grand Ticino or Rocco's, Italian restaurants I am glad to find still there. Rosa Wells, the friend with the apartment, recalled that once she and Eudora sat talking on a park bench, Eudora relating stories. Looking up, they saw that a crowd of total strangers had gathered and were listening eagerly.

Eudora was in Chapel Hill in 1986 to speak on Louis Rubin's retirement. I took her to the airport, some fifteen miles or more away. When nearly there she found she had forgotten her bag, left it behind at the Carolina Inn. A quick stop, a rapid call. Yes, they had found it. Yes, they would dispatch it by messenger. But time was short. Already tired from her many engagements while with us, she became very nervous and upset. The bag arrived at the airport entrance with only scant minutes to spare. The designated gate for her flight was the most distant one. I sprinted ahead, while she, already hampered with arthritis, proceeded slowly behind. I meant to try and hold the plane. Suddenly, from behind me came a little beeping honk, and Eudora swept by on one of the airport conveyances, driven by a beaming black man. Her humor and balance quite restored, she waved at me. "Hop on, dearie!" she cried. The last I saw of her she was passing through the gate, the last one on, but making it, as one had always to be sure she would.

When Eudora's parents moved to Mississippi before she was born, they were soon to present a most happy gift to that much burdened and blemished society. For ninety years she has blessed us, and in view of the rich work she has left us, we can continue to be grateful forever.

ELIZABETH SPENCER

—≈—

XXII

Clerihews

Dear Eudora,

When you had your seventy-fifth birthday, I wrote some celebratory clerihews, and since I then used up all the possible rhymes for your name, I hope that you won't mind my repeating those clerihews on your ninetieth, which I do with greetings and undiminished affection,

—Dick

When Eudora Welty
Published her *Racconti Scelti*
Italy exclaimed with one voice
That her stories were choice.

Eudora

Is admired in Ireland, begorrah,

Having entered the literary scene

With a book called *Curtain of Green.*

Eudora

Excels in the short stora,

And also displays strength

In fictions of greater length.

Eudora

Employs an amphora

(Her name being Greek)

To fetch branch-water from the creek.

Eudora

Does not have a pet remora.

Alas, remoras appear to

Require a shark to adhere to.

Eudora

Seldom visits Zamora.

Nor does Liechtenstein excite her.

She is a regional writer.

Eudora,

If you are looking fora,

Can be found in her usual seat

In the window on Pinehurst Street.

RICHARD WILBUR

—∞—

Contributors

RICHARD BAUSCH, a member of the Fellowship of Southern Writers, is a novelist and short story writer. His most recent novel is *Good Evening Mr. & Mrs. America, and All the Ships at Sea* (1997). He has a volume of stories, *The Selected Stories of Richard Bausch* (1996) published as a Modern Library edition, as does Eudora Welty.

DORIS BETTS is a celebrated and much honored novelist, short story writer, teacher at the University of North Carolina at Chapel Hill, and member of the Fellowship of Southern Writers. Her works include the story collection, *Beasts of the Southern Wild and Other Stories* (1973), and her most recent novel, *The Sharp Teeth of Love* (1997).

FRED CHAPPELL defies being categorized by genre by excelling in them all. Poet, novelist, short story writer, essayist, critic, teacher, and above all, reader. Chappell is a founding member of the Fellowship of Southern Writers. His novels include *It Is Time, Lord* (1963) and most recently *Farewell, I'm Bound to Leave You* (1996).

ELLEN DOUGLAS, a Mississippi novelist and member of the Fellowship of Southern Writers, has most recently published *Truth: Four Stories I Am Finally Old Enough to Tell* (1998). Douglas, also a highly regarded teacher, lives in Jackson, Mississippi.

TONY EARLEY, author of the short story collection *Here We Are in Paradise* (1994), has had stories selected for publication in numerous

115

editions of both *Best American Short Stories* and *New Stories from the South*. He has been awarded a PEN Syndicated Fiction Award and a National Magazine Award for his stories.

CLYDE EDGERTON and his wife Susan Ketchin shared the Eudora Welty Chair of Southern Letters at Millsaps College in 1996. Edgerton is a member of the Fellowship of Southern Writers and the author of several novels, including *Raney* (1985), *Walking Across Egypt* (1987), and *Where Trouble Sleeps* (1997).

GEORGE GARRETT has authored more than twenty-five books and edited another seventeen. His highly praised novel *Death of the Fox* was published in 1971. Garrett's latest book of short stories, academic anecdotes and essays, *Bad Man Blues: A Portable George Garrett* (1998), proves he is a renaissance man and confirms why he is a member of the Fellowship of Southern Writers.

ELLEN GILCHRIST, once a student in Eudora Welty's class at Millsaps College, has written a dozen short story collections and novels including *In the Land of Dreamy Dreams* (1981), *Net of Jewels* (1992), and *Flights of Angels* (1998).

ANTHONY GROOMS, a poet and short story writer, teaches at Kennesaw State University. *Trouble No More: Stories* won the Lillian Smith Book Award for fiction (1996).

BARRY HANNAH, a native Mississippian and long time writer-in-residence at the University of Mississippi, continues to shatter conventions with his stories and novels. His latest story collections include *Bats Out of Hell* (1992) and *High Lonesome* (1996).

MARY HOOD'S two story collections *How Far She Went*, winner of the Flannery O'Connor Award for Short Fiction (1984), and *Venus Is Blue* (1986) are filled with unforgettable characters. Her first novel is titled *Familiar Heat* (1995). Hood has also received a Whiting Writers' Award.

GREG JOHNSON has written a novel, *Pagan Babies* (1993), and several short story collections, including *Distant Friends* (1990), and *I Am Dangerous* (1996). He recently published *Invisible Writer* (1998), a biography of Joyce Carol Oates. Johnson, like Welty, has won the O. Henry Prize Award.

WILLIAM MAXWELL, a novelist and fiction editor at the *New Yorker* from 1936-1976, is a long-time reader and friend of Eudora Welty's. He is the author of numerous books, including *So Long, See You Tommorrow* (1980) and *All the Days and Nights: The Collected Stories of William Maxwell* (1995). Maxwell wrote the foreword for Welty's *One Time, One Place* (1971).

WILLIE MORRIS, former editor of *Harper's*, is a novelist and memoirist who grew up in Yazoo, Mississippi and now resides in Jackson. His works include the autobiographical *North Toward Home* (1967) and *New York Days* (1993). Morris shares the honor of being a recipient of the Richard Wright Medal for Literary Excellence with Eudora Welty.

ALICE MUNRO, Canadian fiction writer, has stunned and pleased readers with her stories for thirty years—from *Dance of the Happy Shades* (1968) to *The Love of a Good Woman* (1998). During her distinguished career, she has been the recipient of three Governor General's Literary Awards, Canada's highest honor for fiction.

DANIÈLE PITAVY-SOUQUES of Dijon, France, introduced European readers to the power of Welty's fiction with her study *La Mort de Méduse* (1992) and was instrumental in Welty's being honored with the award of the Chevalier des Arts et Lettres (1987), the Docteur Honoris Causa of the University of Burgundy (1993), and the Chevalier de la Légion d'Honneur (1996).

REYNOLDS PRICE, long time friend of Eudora Welty's and fellow member of the Fellowship of Southern Writers, has published volumes of novels, plays, poems, memoirs, nonfiction, and short stories, including *Kate Vaiden* (1986), winner of the National Book Critics Award , *Collected Stories* (1993), and *Collected Poems* (1997).

LOUIS D. RUBIN, JR., a founding member of the Fellowship of Southern Writers, has always been a leader in the recognition, encouragement, teaching, publication, and posterity of Southern letters. In 1982 he founded the publishing house, Algonquin Books of Chapel Hill. Rubin is the author and editor of over forty books, including the novels, *The Golden Weather* (1961) and *The Heat of the Sun* (1995).

LEE SMITH, generous as both student and teacher, has written more than a dozen novels and story collections, including *Cakewalk* (1980), *Fair and Tender Ladies* (1988), and *News of the Spirit* (1997). In 1991, she received the first Chubb LifeAmerica Award in honor of Robert Penn Warren from the Fellowship of Southern Writers.

WILLIAM JAY SMITH who has written more than fifty volumes of poems, including *Collected Poems 1939–1989* (1990), and *The World Below the Window: Poems 1937–1997* (1998), has been a friend of Eudora Welty's for more than fifty years. Among his honors and awards is the distinction of being Professor Emeritus of English at Hollins College.

ELIZABETH SPENCER of Mississippi, Italy, Canada, and North Carolina is a member of the Fellowship of Southern Writers. She is the author of numerous novels and volumes of short stories including *Ship Island and Other Stories* (1968), which she dedicted to Eudora Welty, and *Collected Stories* (1981). Spencer and Welty enjoy a long professional and personal friendship.

RICHARD WILBUR won the Pulitzer Prize in poetry for *Things of this World: Poems* (1956), and served as Poet Laureate of the United States (1987–88). He is also a distinguished teacher and a member of the American Academy of Arts and Letters, an honor also bestowed upon Eudora Welty.